A Fast Bike
to North
Cape

Andy C Wareing

Copyright

Andy C Wareing

Cover design by Andy C Wareing

CONTENTS

To Georgie and Ella—Prost! Wherever you may be.

A Crash

The storm seemed to have no earthly bounds. It was the hunger cry of a thousand ravenous wolves. The wind tore horizontally across the tundra. It howled with an intense fury that tore and shredded my senses. The gale snagged at the edges of my clothing. It pushed and pulled me as I staggered blindly to my knees. The rain was a dirty cold mix of sleet and ice, a hard and stinging blast, it swept in sheets across the frozen landscape.

Muddy water had obscured my visor but when I raised it with a numbed and shaking hand in an attempt to see, the blizzard blinded me entirely and disoriented, I fell back with a groan of despair, pain and frustration into the water filled gully.

I pulled the visor back down and smeared a peep hole in the mud with the back of a rain sodden leather glove. Lying on my back I looked up at the sky. Low clouds, so close I felt that I could reach out and snatch them from the sky flew like an angry murmuration above me, the day so dark it might have been midnight.

"Land of the fucking midnight sun my hairy biker's arse," I muttered.

I lay there for a full minute, panting and taking stock but then, over the whine and cry of the wind I heard the engine of my precious Kawasaki, still running, a quickly ascending drone of destruction. I crawled to my hands and knees and peered out of the gully to see my bike lying on its side only twenty feet away. The engine was running and still in second gear, the rear wheel was digging itself ruinously into the side of the permafrost mud bank. The engine note was a high whine, adding its ruinous voice to the banshee wail of the storm.

I staggered back to my feet and lumbered heavily across the terrain. It was a challenge in motorcycle boots, winded as I was. Clumps of frozen grass and weed, formed mounds and icy moguls to snare ankles and trip the unwary. Deep pools lay hidden beneath shrouds of thick bracken. Icicles coated every surface. My right side hurt badly and as I staggered, I felt for a cracked rib. I looked down to see a tear in the waterproofs and leathers across my right shoulder and finally the heat of adrenalin seeped away to be replaced by relief and trembling icy shock.

The next few minutes were a blur. I staggered and slipped. I rose for a moment to my feet, but the ferocity of the wind blew me over. I shuffled like a toddler on all fours through the mud and the permafrost, freezing cold, soaked, sick with pain and wild disorientation, always drawn by the whine of the bike.

Finally, I fell face first into a rain filled gully, hard against the familiar black fairing and hard petrol tank of my bike. I let out a wild shout of exultation and pain and leant across to hit the kill switch.

I heard some voices and turned to see that some cars had stopped and a few of their more foolhardy and adventurous occupants were making their way cautiously across the difficult terrain towards me.

"Hei! Er du ok?" Called out a voice in Norwegian.

I waved to let them know that I was OK but also that I still needed some assistance.

I looked for Georgie and Ella. I scanned the horizon for a sign of his black helmet or Ella's orange one-piece waterproof, but they were nowhere to be seen and my stomach flipped, and my heart sank.

I got beside the bike and with one hand on the left handlebar and one on the frame close to the engine I tried to right it, but with the mud and the weight of all of my luggage it just slid and pivoted on the cracked part of the fairing where it had landed. Then I was surrounded by four or five strangers, soaked to their skins, dressed incongruously in jeans and t-shirts, come to help the crazy Englishman with the crashed motorcycle.

I was six-hundred miles inside the Arctic Circle, three-thousand miles from home and, given the chance, or the rub of a lamp, I would have wished to have literally been anywhere else at that moment. But where the hell where Georgia and Ella?

A Crossing

P ins and needles tingled my numbed feet, too hot and sweaty inside my too tight motorcycle boots. The heavy vibration felt through the reclining chair bolted to the steel floor had never left me. From the moment we had slipped our moorings in Newcastle in the North-East of England, until the moment my eyes had been forced open by the first grey kiss of light that broke free of the horizon, I had been constantly jiggled and shook by the reverberations of the heavy diesel engines of the MV Jupiter, the Fjord Lines ferry that was slowly bringing me closer to the shoreline of Norway.

The overnight ferry journey had been arduous. A twelve-hour long slog through dark and heaving seas. A rough sailing through shipping areas that still recalled more comfortable times as a young boy at home; times sat bathed in the yellow valve light of the old radio with my Dad; he listening to the evening shipping weather forecast on BBC Radio 4, me, eyes heavy, pretending I wasn't sleepy at all, so that I could spend a few more minutes sat on his comfortable lap, smelling his distinctive scent of tobacco and Brylcreem. So evocative to me that if I smell it even now, a long lifetime later, I still turn to look for his so familiar face.

The announcer's voice seeping from the airwaves, a BBC plum in his throat, a tone of voice slow and melodic, a hypnotist's cadence.

"German Bight, Viking. Southeast veering southwest 4 or 5, occasionally 6 later. Thundery showers. Moderate or good, occasionally poor. Tyne, Dogger. Northeast 3 or 4. Occasional rain. Moderate or poor."

As we crawled across the North Sea, we had sailed through all of the old poetically redolent names for the shipping areas located in the North Sea around the United Kingdom, all as I had tried, mostly in vain, to sleep.

The problem had not been the discomfort or the constant roll of the ship. The problem had been the extremely boisterous gang of thirty or so Norwegian boys in the ship's bar. Booze was cheap on the ship, and they were returning home to Norway where the price of alcohol,

and pretty much everything else, was extortionate in comparison. The Norsemen were drunkenly, and loudly intent on making the most of the discount prices. From the
time the ship had slipped its moorings until the sun had
risen, they had made the most of the opportunity given to
them. They were dressed in pastel-coloured sweaters and
wore loafers, young and clean cut, they were probably all
accountants and banking assistants back home, but the
booze had transformed them into Viking marauders. Red
faced and belligerent they shouted and sang at the tops
of their voices, and nobody on the ship was willing to
challenge them.

I just hoped a few of them had remained sufficiently
sober to drive them to wherever their home might lie.

The bell chimed softly to let us stretching, and yawning
second class passengers know that the dining room was
open for service. We were seated on the upper deck of the
ferry, in rows of chairs like airline passengers, uncomfortable because a cabin was beyond our simple means. We
righted ourselves from our reclined postures by moving
the back of the chair forwards an eighth of an inch, and
with cracking limbs we rose like sleepwalkers to stumble
across to the line of windows that gave egress to the first
sight of our destination.

The sky had brightened even as the sun struggled to break free of the dark purpling bruise of clouds that clung to the horizon, intent on hanging onto the security of the night. To starboard, a line of rough green hills hove into view, granite escarpments dotted with red and yellow timbered buildings. My heart raced; my stomach churned; my first sight of Norway.

It always felt this way, and I hope with all of my soul that it always will. That initial glimpse of somewhere alien, the scorching burn of the thrill and the cold chill of the anxiety of the unknown. An entirely new world. A foreign culture, an unknown language, a puzzling currency, and a few thousand miles to travel. Each fresh mile stretching out with the threat and the promise of bringing to me all of the adventure that I craved.

My thoughts were interrupted by the press of passengers heading to the dining room, so I walked to the bathroom, had a quick pee, and ran shockingly cold water through my thinning hair, doused the last of the sleep from my red, aching eyes and joined them.

The ferry operator was Norwegian and so, therefore, was the food. No greasy bacon, fried bread, black pudding, and sausages for me that morning. I forked some smoked salmon and scrambled eggs onto some rye bread. Took two apples and two bread rolls and a pile of salami and sat by a starboard window to watch the coastline roll by. The shore was dark and forbidding. Stunted trees grew from rocky outcrops. Meadow stretched from sandy beach to be suddenly interrupted by a towering eruption of cliff.

Fingers of land crawled like tendrils into the sea, sparkled by the rising sun into a thousand gemstones. Small bays and rolling hills were obscured by a sky so low it became, at times, difficult to discern where the land ended, and the sky began. The windows of the ferry were bathed in a watery sun and then lashed by a sudden squall that swept in horizontally across the white flecked sea.

I ate the salmon and scrambled egg and wrapped the rolls and salami into a napkin, and along with the apples secreted them into my helmet. It was time to descend into the bowels of the loading bay and make sure my bike was OK and prepared for the day. The rain was a disappointment. I was tired and had a long ride ahead of me. I had hoped for better weather. I was deeply aware of the long journey, ferry lag I suppose, a slower and yet no less inexorably fatiguing experience.

By the side of the bike, I pulled out my one-piece waterproof outfit, a giant rustling black and red condom of a thing and pulled it on over my boots and shrugged it on over the shoulders of my old and familiar leather jacket. I pulled on my beloved Lem 3 helmet and cinched up the chin strap good and tight.

With lunch safely deposited in my trusty tank bag I checked that the map for Bergen and all ways north was visible. Amid the other drivers I sat astride my bike just as the klaxon rang and I felt the motion of the ship first churn as the engines were reversed and then the bump and shimmy as the ship was pulled, hawser tight against the dock.

Butterflies fluttered as the heavy loading door was slowly and noisily winched down. I felt like a British Commando intent upon a dawn assault upon the beaches of Normandy. The heavy mechanical winches clanged out a drumbeat descent that signalled our assault upon the shore.

The cold rain of a new dawn in a new land swept into the cargo bay. All of Scandinavia lay waiting for me, a long jagged, fjord filled finger of mystery and adventure ahead. I pulled my visor down, checked my gloves were tight, pulled in the clutch, pressed the engine start button, and cogged the bike into first gear. It was time for this pale Anglo-Saxon to get some revenge for the Viking raids against my ancient ancestors. With a blip of the throttle, the exhaust barked, a Viking battle cry of my own, I set off up the long and greasy ramp, up out of the dank hold and into the bright grey day to pit myself against this fresh and exciting adversary.

BERGEN

The year I rode off that ferry and into the damp environs of Bergen, it was 1989 and I was twenty-four years old. The world was changing rapidly around me. Communism was coming to an end; the Berlin wall would soon fall. George W H Bush had just become the 41st president of the United States and the internet was just about to be birthed.

After my long and lonely ride to Istanbul ended, as told in '*A Fast Bike to Byzantium*,' for the next couple of years I decided to test out the staying power and resilience of a few girlfriends by tormenting and torturing them on the back of a fast and deeply uncomfortable motorcycle. Of course, none of them were up to the punishing mileage, tiny, cramped tent, severely limited luggage capabilities and the extremes of weather that I would voluntarily subject myself to.

They all failed to stay the distance. Italy, Germany, the south of France, these were all easy destinations, tourist hot spots compared to where I would normally ride, but still, not one turned out to be a keeper. Not even close.

And so it was, not too surprisingly, that I was solo again. I had tired of easy strolls through Europe and wanted something more challenging. I had spent hours poring over maps and wondering what distant target I could hit on an extreme budget and get safely back home within the three-week window afforded to me by my employer in the UK.

I considered Morocco. A ride through Spain to reach the northern part of the Sahara. Casablanca, Marrakesh, names filled with mystique and mystery. An African odyssey. Or perhaps a ride through Italy to take a ferry from the toe of Sicily to reach Tunisia and a ride east along the coast to Egypt.

And then one rainy night, with not enough money in my pocket to go meet my mates for even a single pint, I was watching TV when a short Norwegian film came on. It had English subtitles and was called '*Nordkapp – The Land of the Midnight Sun.*' The film showed a land mass rearing one-thousand feet out of a heaving sea, sheer cliffs of iron hard rock, all set beneath a sun that simply refused to set. An island, the northern most tip of Europe, deep inside the Arctic Circle.

I immediately opened my set of European road maps and unfolded them on my mum's kitchen table. Always the location of some of my worst decisions. My finger traced the potential route. Initially across the sea to Bergen and then a convoluted route around and across fjords. Ferries, mountain passes and across frozen permafrost encrusted tundra all the way up the remote island of Magerøya that sat like a frozen gem in the distant arctic sea. And then to travel as far north as it was possible to do and still remain in Europe. Nordkapp. North Cape.

And then back through Finland and Sweden and into Denmark before finding a route home. I might even stop off in Holland and visit an old friend of mine for a beer or two.

A four-thousand-mile round trip, without a single word of any of the Nordic languages in my vocabulary, seven countries, four of which I had never previously travelled to, challenging riding conditions all the way, dreadful weather. It ticked all the boxes. I was in.

I decided that the Suzuki GS1000G I had used to ride through the Iron Curtain had been both too comfortable and not quite quick enough. A new bike was being advertised as the fastest production street bike you could buy. It came available soon after the film Top Gun was released and Tom Cruise, as Maverick, rode the Kawasaki GPZ900R to the soundtrack 'Highway to the Danger Zone.' The bike I craved was the GPZ900R's even bigger and faster brother and I desperately wanted one. It was the Kawasaki GPZ1000RX.

So, on one grey rainy day I rode to Manchester in the north-west of England. Of course, every day is a rainy day in Manchester, it is a perennially gloomy city, bordered as it is by the hills of the Pennines to the north and east. At the motorcycle dealers in Salford, I traded in my trusty Suzuki in exchange for a black GPZ1000RX. For the time it was astoundingly fast and handled like nothing I had ridden before, low clip-on handlebars and aggressive rear set foot pegs, it reeked street racer and I loved it.

Of course, it was also wildly uncomfortable in the way that only sport motorcycles can be. The narrow hard seat, perfect for carving turns on a track, felt much like a brick thrown to the nethers after only a few miles. The riding position pitched me forwards and was heavy on the wrists, a carpal tunnel syndrome inducing ache. But I didn't care a jot. All the way home I looked for reflective shop windows to check out how I looked on my new beauty. Together we were wicked fast and, at least with my full-face helmet on, I thought we looked amazing. The bike looked cool anyway, which I fervently and desperately believed made me look cool by proxy, and that's all that really mattered to me when I was twenty-four.

As I rode up the slick ramp and into that cold grey morning in Bergen, I was immediately reminded of the poor choices I had made. I stood up on the pegs to adjust my down below man parts and shook the pins and needles from my wrists. But the bike burbled reassuringly underneath me, the steering, brakes, and throttle were all smooth and responsive. I felt confident this ride was going to be a breeze.

The roads were damp, and the clouds overhead were pregnant with imminent downpours. I navigated slowly away from the docks, across bridges that spanned railway lines, through commercial districts and underneath large crane gantries busy at construction.

The road ascended steeply into the hills north of the city. It was barely ten in the morning, but it felt like dusk was already settling over the landscape, the cloud was so low it hovered in the tree line like a spectre. The first drop of rain streaked across my visor, then a big fat droplet spattered right between my eyes making me jump and then the heavens opened. The road was old and deeply carved by the use of heavy goods vehicles. Two deep troughs had been worn by decades of use, wagon wheel wide they both quickly filled with a filthy sluice of rainwater.

I was forced to either ride, precariously balanced on the highly cambered mound of dryish tarmac in the centre of the road, or to pick a trough, left or right, and carve through the standing water like a speedboat, leaving a frothing white wake in my mirrors.

The trucks, either leaving the docks laden with piles of broken concrete and tortured limbs of rusting steel or heading back towards the construction sites dotted around Bergen with pallets of cement and breeze blocks only exacerbated matters. They ploughed carelessly through the furrows sending torrents of water high into the air, it was like riding through a murky fish tank. The air itself was sodden, I expected to see Nemo swim out of a resin pirate ship beside a volcano spewing oxygen bubbles.

Mile after mile we climbed, my only guides the red taillights of the trucks in front of me, blurred like a Gerhard Richter painting. It was wretched and I was soon soaked despite the supposedly waterproof over suit. The rainwater permeated my gloves, was driven by the wind up my sleeves, it seeped down my collars and penetrated the seams by my boots and then, osmosis like, crawled up the hem of my jeans to soak me as high as my knees.

It was wretched and very dangerous. Every now and again I slipped from my high ground into one of the flooded furrows. The bike swerved and twitched, shimmied, and slipped sideways like a rider on a log flume, until I could find time, white knuckled, to power out back onto my little middle mound.

It was only when I entered the Selvik and Glaskar tunnels close to the town of Ervik, little arched entry ways, like railway tunnels beneath a granite outcrop, that the rain relented, and the road lost its twin furrows. The articulated lorries and trucks had slowly dissipated as I had journeyed north, they, turning off the main road to reach quarries and supply depots in the hills. They finally left me alone, and as I rode across a little bridge close to the small town of Lyngholmen that crossed the inlet of Hjelmåsvågen a parking area opened up on my right and the sun finally broke free of the heavy rolling clouds.

I pulled over, parked the bike and took off the waterproof over suit. I was wetter than an otter's pocket, but the view was spectacular, everything I had hoped Norway would be. The inlet was shaped like a teardrop. Surrounded by rearing pines, a small redwood boathouse stood at the water's edge. A jagged peak, a shark's tooth crest of grey granite rose to tower over the distant vista. The low clouds burned slowly away, and as I pulled out my stolen buns and salami, a hint of blue sky peeped shyly out between marshmallow cushions. Where the land ended and the water began was impossible to discern, a Bob Ross impossibly still reflection.

I took a photo while I sat munching my dry lunch, steaming in the warming rays of the sunshine, and marvelling at the prefect symmetry of sky and inland sea. It is the photo that adorns the front cover of this book that you hold in your hands, and it will always remind me of that morning's first adventurous footfalls that quickly immersed me into the stunning, all surrounding vistas of Norway. The memory of that familiar, gut wrenching feeling of being entirely alone in a new and strange country.

The first step had been made. Thousands remaining. The trembling friction of that first tentative day of the plan, long conceived, now to be committed.

I spent the rest of the day carving around sweeping bends, across small inlets, around boatyards and across bridges. The sun followed my progress and my waterproofs remained on the back of the bike. My gloves and boots slowly dried in the weak sunshine.

Dotted along the road were large white clapboard houses with tin roofs. The road was smooth and fast, at times it carved through the fern covered granite that stood like sentinels, tall on either side of me. The hills were a mesh of low cedar, Norway Spruce and towering Scots pine, the air was suffused with the fresh nasal stinging scent that Febreze and Glade would sell their souls to replicate.

For admirers of Douglas Adams and The Hitchhikers Guide to the Galaxy this, of course, was the part of Norway created by the fictional character Slartibartfast, the planet architect who won an award for 'all of the lovely crinkly edges.' It is fjords everywhere, a constant crossing of inlets and lakes, pine covered hills, high bluffs, cliffs and more inlets and lakes. It was a wonderful ride on the bike, but, as the day wore ever on, it began to feel like I was really getting nowhere. The roads headed north for a few miles and then looped back around to circumnavigate another vast and shimmering lake. I was taken miles away from the route a crow would measure just to cross a tiny bridge across a narrow inlet. I could often see the road I needed, lying only a few metres across a pristine lake, but it might take me twenty or thirty minutes of admittedly fun riding to get there.

It was late afternoon when I saw the sign for my first ferry crossing at 'Oppedal ferjekai.' I admit to being very excited. This first ferry would take me just three miles across the huge sea inlet to the town of Lavik. The inlet was sheltered and calm and the ferry was loaded with the greatest efficiency. There was only me and perhaps fourteen or fifteen cars. I put the bike on the centre stand and bought a coffee from the small onboard shop just as we slipped our moorings and took to the open water.

I sat close to the prow, jacket open to the sea breeze sipping my coffee. I was still a little damp around the edges and ahead I could see dark clouds piling up against the lee of the distant hills, but the views everywhere were spectacular. The sea was immense and flat calm with gentle eddies stirred by hidden currents. Every hill and peak was wreathed in cloud that spilled slowly down to the water's edge like ice water running down a gully. Small smacks, fishing boats, were returning from the days fishing beyond the shelter of the fjord. They cut arrows in the water, ripples that ran across the surface until they were depleted and vanished at the water's edge.

As we pulled into the dock at Lavik, the rain began to patter and so, with a sigh, I pulled on my black and red ill-fitting condom suit and rustled my way noisily back across to the Kawasaki. By the time we disembarked, the rain was a steady pelt, and the light was beginning to leach from the sky. It was much too early for dusk, the weight of the cloud simply occluded all of the light from the sky, my world became Tupperware grey. I decided to look for a camp.

I found what I was looking for by the side of a stretch of water with an unpronounceable name. The site only had a tiny shop and a small toilet block with a single shower, but it was pretty, seated as it was on a sandy beach that sloped down to the cold expanse of the lake. I was too tired to keep looking for anything bigger and better equipped. I checked out the shop and realized that I couldn't afford...anything really. The beers were three times what I was used to paying in the UK, so I spent a week's wages on a large carton of eggs, put up my little tent in the gentle rain and set my little gas stove to boil the eggs in some bone achingly cold water from the lake.

I had brought my little Sony Walkman cassette player with me, so while I waited for the water to boil, I found it and the compilation tape secreted away in the bottom of my panniers. Soon INXS's Michael Hutchence singing '*Never Tear us Apart*' and T'Pau's Carol Decker banging out '*China in your Hands*' was ringing out around the empty campsite.

Night slipped its cold cloak around my shoulders. I wasn't yet so far north that my proximity to the Arctic Circle made any significant difference to the time of the sunset; I was still at a line of latitude similar to the Scottish Shetland Isles. Regardless, the cloud cover had long since thrown a funereal shroud over what little light remained from the setting of the sun, and all of the stars remained hidden. I was already feeling lonely. I was damp and tired and a little depressed.

And then, I looked around to see that the darkness across the campsite was almost complete. The only sound was the wind high in the tops of the firs and the water lapping gently on the shore of the lake. The faintest chink of moonlight broke through the dense clouds to create a silhouette of my bike outside my tent. It was a reassurance. Tomorrow would bring new roads and new discoveries. Good or bad. It didn't matter to me. What a life. One man and his bike, alone with his music, his boiled eggs, and his thoughts.

A Dilemma

The ethereal light of the cold new day slowly grew to softly illuminate the inside of my little, cramped tent. I sat upright for a few minutes, in my unnervingly damp sleeping bag, in the already musty smelling tent, rubbing the sleep from my eyes and stretching the kinks out of my back. I didn't have a mattress of any sort, it wouldn't fit on the bike, so I was, with the exception of the padding of the sleeping bag, effectively sleeping on the beneficence of the thick Norwegian grass and fern frond covered ground.

The sleeping bag was warm, but my breath steamed in the cold morning air. I thought about the previous day and all of the miles ahead of me while I pushed the confusion of sleep from my mind.

Bergen had not been what I had expected. Much busier, much more industrial. I guess in my young mind I had envisioned some pastel-coloured fishing huts nestled around an azure fjord, where Arran jumpered fishermen called out to each other from jaunty sailboats in a language forever alien and obscure to me. Of course, Bergen had failed to live up to that overly romanticized ideal. After all, it is a bustling metropolis of a quarter of a million people.

I now know that the Bergen of my dreams does exist, the Møhlenpris, Sandviken, and Loddefjord districts are beautiful, but I had arrived by ferry and only seen the ferry terminal and the main road out, and just like airports, ferry terminals generally place you in the heart of the industrialized parts of the city. Seldom do you get off a ferry or exit an airport to find yourself surrounded by culture and fine dining options. More typically its McDonalds, tire outlets and strip joints, and so it had been with my first taste of Norway.

But I had enjoyed the ride after I managed to escape the environs of the city, and the bike had performed flawlessly, even in the fishbowl-filled gullies of the surrounding hills. In the heavy rain, I had worried the bike's carburettors and ignition system might become saturated and start to misfire, but the Kawasaki had done great—hadn't missed a single beat.

I pulled on a fresh t-shirt and shrugged into my leather jacket and struggled into jeans, awkward in the confines of the tent. I reached for my blue and red striped Frank Thomas riding boots. They were as snazzy and de-rigueur for the era in the same way that the music of Wham and George Michael's bouffant hairstyle matched the fundamental joy and feeling of the times I travelled through. Unfortunately, the boots were already, like much of the rest of me, very damp. I sat with my legs outside of the tent and slipped my wrinkled feet into them with a grimace.

I sloshed and squelched my way down to the edge of the lake to get some water in order to brew some coffee. An eerie mist hung close to the cold water of the perfectly still lake. I looked up to see a large grey heron stood serenely in the shallows watching me. Grebes, shrouded by the mist far out on the water shrilled and shouted. In the far distance, three craggy, glacier-carved peaks reached into the cold morning sky, their reflections reaching out across the mirror of the water towards me. The heron sensed my proximity and lumbered into the sky on arcing wings, three toes on each foot dragging through the water and leaving behind diverging ripples that fractured the pristine surface of the lake.

Even today, forty-something years later, I only have to close my eyes and I am back there. Stood stock still. Mouth comically agape as I held my breath in quiet awe at the beauty of the scene. I can feel the bite of the cold morning air. I can smell the grass and hear once again the profound silence that enveloped me like a comforting blanket.

Back at the tent with my little Billycan sloshing with water, I found the campsite to be desolate, and the road empty, not a single car to be seen. I could have been the last soul alive. I had another cold boiled egg for breakfast and while I waited for my gas stove to slowly raise the water temperature for my coffee from glacial to tepid, I reached over to unzip the tank bag and retrieve my Michelin map.

I sat cross-legged outside my tent, sipping lukewarm coffee, tracing the thin lines of potential routes for today's ride across my folded map. My campsite was a little north of Lavik, and the distance I had covered the previous day looked impressive. At least until I unfolded several large pages of the map to display the full length of Norway and took the time to calculate the number of miles I had covered the previous day. In nearly four hours of riding, I had only covered a little over one hundred miles. As I sat, my mouth agape, the vast peninsula of Norway stretched out ahead of me like a long and jagged finger of doom, and in that moment, I admit, I despaired.

The task seemed impossible. At least one-thousand three hundred more miles lay ahead of me to even reach

Nordkapp, and I had to allow sufficient time to ride back home again. I was on a strict time budget. I was as far from being a wealthy adventurer with limitless time at his disposal as it was possible to be. I only had so many days off work, and I wasn't sure what other challenges and obstacles might lie ahead of me. For the first time, at the very beginning of a journey, I suddenly wondered why on earth I was doing this to myself. I felt like just giving up the destination and the dream at once. I had no real reason to ride to the northernmost part of Europe other than it was the northernmost part of Europe.

Then I thought back to the ferry of the previous day. The three-mile ferry journey had robbed me of more than forty-five minutes. A full hour if I added in the fifteen minutes that I had to wait for the thing to arrive. My original plan had been to explore the fjords of the west coast using the ferries that allowed riders to circumnavigate the more broken and fragmented areas splintered by the ancient glaciers that penetrated deeply into the countryside.

But based on yesterday's experience I simply didn't have the luxury of the time that that would entail. I looked again at the map. The alternative was to ride almost due north and head into the mountains, into the very heart of Norway and away from the coast I desperately wanted to explore and experience.

It was a real dilemma.

I knew that heading west would provide the finer scenery, more rural fishing villages, the Norway of my dreams, but I was also aware that more fjords meant more ferries, and while they were enjoyable and incredibly scenic, they were painfully slow.

With a sigh of resignation, I realized that, back at mum's kitchen table, with my maps and scattered pieces of paper all around me with notes and calculations jotted across them, I had miscalculated badly. If I had had the luxury of a time machine and access to Google Maps, the route planner software would have quickly and easily told me that the path I desperately wanted to take was simply not viable. I had had to find out the hard way by putting feet and tires on the hard ground. I had assumed, while my dear old Mum fussed around me and brought me yet another cup of tea and wondered if she was ever going to get her kitchen table back, that the ferries I needed would be moored up waiting for me when I rolled up and then they would whisk me across a pretty stretch of water at the same average speed I was making on the GPZ.

Of course, that had turned out to be very far from reality. I had to average much more than the three miles an hour the ferries were giving me. At that pace I could simply push the bike to Nordkapp faster and save a few thousand Krona on fuel.

A compromise needed to be made. I could either abandon my plans to reach the northern most of Europe, and instead, enjoy a lazy, easy week or so of exploring the west coast. Or I could head inland and roll back the throttle and eat some miles. Push the bike and myself hard and still get to the Arctic Circle.

I decided to seek out the mountains. It was the only way I could accomplish the goal of reaching and experiencing the wonder of Nordkapp and the midnight sun. That, after all, had always been my original plan. My goal and my only real reason for being here.

It was mid-July and while I expected to see some snow on this trip, the highest peak I would encounter would top out at only seven-thousand feet. I would ride north towards the town of Førde before turning eastwards towards the Tafjordfjella mountain range, now part of the 760 square mile Reinheimen National Park close to the Jostedalsbreen glacier and then onwards, always snaking my way torturously north, towards the town of Vegset before looking for a campsite.

It would be a very long day's ride, but the tightly packed contours of the map suggested it would be through some spectacular scenery and, if all went to plan, it would put me back on track. So, with a small smile of both resignation and a resolve renewed, I folded up my map and slipped it back into its compartment on the tank bag. I rolled up my sleeping bag and packed my tent and few sparse cooking items, stretched, and mentally prepared myself for the day.

A Glacier

With the bike packed, I pulled on a dry sweater and, making sure my waterproofs were to hand, I set off. The roads were quiet and smooth. Northern Europe and Scandinavia are a joy to ride a motorcycle in. Well laid tarmac, not too many slippery grids or iron manhole covers on the racing line, predictable cambers and bends that carve on for eternity.

The bike felt wonderful. We swooped through the bends together, pulled mile after mile under us. Every touch of the throttle made the bike surge forwards, keen to please every request my eager wrist signalled. My eyes were narrowed, always looking at my entry and exit to every gorgeous bend that just kept coming. The throaty burble from the exhaust was a joy to my ears, we were flying, man and machine joined in joyous synchrony. Sheer cliffs of granite towered on one side, cold fathomless lakes the perfect colour of the sky on the other. Through forests of pine and by the side of chuckling brooks, the panoramas unfolded like the pages of a National Geographic calendar.

I hit a series of hairpins on the southside of the town of Førde. Flowing left and then right, leaning from one side of the bike to the other, powering through the turns with a smile on my face, touching the yellow line in the centre of the road and then cutting the edge of the tarmac just before it gave way to scrub. I was having too much fun and entered the last one far too fast and the right-hand foot peg touched down even as I could see the bend tightening even more. I gave out a little squeal of concern and fought the instinct to grab the front brake. Instead, I leant in further, and counter steered more to get the bike turned and made it round safely with a sigh of relief. A warning to take it a little easier—duly noted.

As we approached the city limits of Førde itself I got behind a Saab 9-3. The driver was sticking rigidly to the speed limit of 50mph and, as the buildings of the approaching town began to rise around us, I tucked in behind him. He seemed to be a competent driver and I knew that he had seen me, with my headlight on, as he had glanced in his rear-view mirror several times. But at exactly the same time that we passed the 30mph sign the driver of the SAAB slammed on his brakes. With a manly shriek and a panicked fistful of front brake, the rear wheel came off the ground and I nearly ran into the back of him.

This was peculiar behaviour to somebody from the UK, especially in the late 1980s. Of course, most motorists slowed down for towns and sort of, kind of, almost adhered to speed limits, but we did it eventually, in a more casual manner. The Norwegians took these speed limits really seriously.

I saw the same behaviour again and again from motorists, I could only assume the police had good radar technology and were more than willing to use it, although on the entire trip I never saw a single, solitary police car.

I saw my first snow covered peak as I pass through the aptly name village of Skei. I was on the outskirts of the Jostedalsbreen National Park, home to the mighty Jostedal Glacier, the largest in continental Europe. The glacier has around fifty branches and its deep ancient blue translucence could be seen lurking in many of the valleys. Unlike many glaciers that remain in that frozen state due to the chilly conditions, the Jostedal glacier almost continually melts but gets topped up, if you will, by heavy annual snowfalls in the mountains at its source.

I stopped for another boiled egg and a drink of water in the mountains. The air carried the chill of the snow that refused to yield and melt in the summer sunshine. A vast snowfield stretched away from me, rent by the jagged granite peaks that pierced it in their assault upon the heavens. I took another picture and as I was putting my Nikon back in the tank bag two other motorcyclists rolled up. They were from Denmark and were well kitted out for touring. One guy was riding a very capable looking Africa Twin and the other rode a BMW R100GS. They had multi-terrain tires and all sorts of kit piled as high as the sun. I glanced across at my RX with its sports bike tires, and low handlebars, with the tiny rack weighed down by a crappy tent and a sleeping bag all rolled up in a bright yellow BT plastic bag and held down by five or six fraying and mismatched bungee cords. I wondered, not for the first time, if I had not considered how tough this ride might turn out to be.

We chatted for a while, and I took the liberty of asking which route they had taken to get to Norway. They had come from the port of Frederikshavn in Denmark to land in Gothenburg in Sweden and then ridden around Oslo to reach where we were now. They were doing what I wanted to do, spending a lazy week catching slow ferries on the west coast. I told them I was heading to Nordkapp and received the usual side eyed expressions and looks of concern and sympathy that I was becoming accustomed to. There was the chill of the snowline in the air, so we shook hands and parted company.

Back on the road I skirted the Jostedalsbreen National Park for much of the afternoon, skimming around bends, watching the tacho needle swing, letting the big Kawasaki have its steam, enjoying the thrill of the scenery and the cold mountain air.

As was typical for all of my trips, I had neglected to carry out much actual research or useful preparation for my trip. Of course, in those days it was much more challenging to do so. In the days before the internet, you either had to either buy a rather dry and informative travel guide written by some boring musty travel writer, or ride the bus into town to browse the non-fiction section of the public library to become at least a little knowledgeable about your planned destination.

I had done neither. I had just picked a destination I had seen a ten-minute film about on the TV. I had selected Nordkaap and set off. So, it was with a jaw dropped by awe that I found myself, in the late afternoon, at the top of the Trollstigen, the Troll Path.

It wasn't particularly well known when I visited in 1989 but today people make it a 'must do' experience to visit and drive the road, a destination a bit like the Road to Hana in Hawaii, The Amalfi coast in Italy or the always splendid joining of the M6 and the M5 at Spaghetti Junction in Birmingham.

The Trollstigen is only open for a few months during the summer and then only to small passenger cars and motorcycles due to the extreme tightness of the turns and the giddying steepness of the descent.

The Trollstigen is a series of eleven hairpins that descend three-thousand feet down an astoundingly steep mountain pass. In England it would be called a cliff. Everywhere you look you are surrounded by forbidding peaks, The Bispen (The Bishop), The Kongen (The King), The Dronninga (The Queen) and to the west The Stigbottshornet and The Storgrovfjellet which seemed to have been named for the challenge of pronunciation rather than anything else. Mighty waterfalls empty into the valley and everywhere is the overpowering, stomach troubling tingle of vertigo.

The first hairpin was a tight right turn and was shockingly lofty. I turned the bike in at the apex and the valley below was revealed to me, like a stage curtain being pulled back. It felt like being on the prow of a ship lofted high into the sky. Snow and clouds mingled at the peaks and the road itself unwound like a grey ribbon below me. The next hairpin was an equally tight left and was within touching distance of two wild surging waterfalls that fell almost vertically from the mass of granite and stone far above me. The water frothed and surged, white water, an elemental release of power from the summit.

Just as the road passed them, the twin streams joined. The wind whipped an icy wild mist from the raging, deafening confluence that immediately soaked me. The spray created an intense, blazing rainbow across the road in front of me. I had never seen such a natural phenomenon so close, so dazzlingly bright and suffused with colour. With a whoop and a holler, I rode directly through it. It was breath-taking.

You have to be careful riding the Trollstigen. The stretches of the road that lie between the hairpins are both long, narrow and steep. It was easy to let the bike's power and momentum lead to too much speed. I was then left with trying to scrub velocity while setting the bike up for a very tight turn with zero run off and a precipice on one side or the other.

After the fifth hairpin I pulled into a little paved area by the side of the road and sat on the bike for a minute or two, panting from the simple focus and the exertion of navigating the pass, while senses were overloaded by dizzying heights, the ferocious roar of the water beneath the bridge and the sight of so many peaks crowded together around the perfect flatness of the valley floor, still a few thousand feet below me.

As I breathlessly reached the valley, the towering mountain peaks teemed suffocatingly around me, it felt like being at the bottom of a vast well. Only a sliver of cloud scudded sky was visible, so lofty and close were the summits. Boulder fields lay strewn across the valley floor. This was truly the land of the trolls of ancient Norse mythology. It didn't take much imagination to envisage furious trolls, driven to insanity by the church bells of the valley, striding from peak to rocky peak uprooting trees and hurling boulders the size of houses from the summits at the passing Christians who taunted them.

In the valley it started to rain again, and I pulled over at an outlook carved into the side of the mountain to catch my breath, take a photo and put my giant rustling prophylactic back on.

Like the road out of Bergen, the air itself soon became saturated. The road quickly filled with water and then the standing rainwater was thrown back by oncoming traffic to join the downpour. My waterproofs were soon overwhelmed. Freezing water soaked through my boots and gloves, rain dripped down the back of my neck. I had the uneasy feeling that my black and red waterproof over suit was actually slowly filling with water. Rather than limiting the ingress, it had become some vast rubber container, bathing me in its increasingly icy contents.

The remainder of that long day was weary despite the scenery that accompanied me. Vast milky lakes, towering vistas, deep valleys cleft between peaks containing madly rushing, boulder tumbling rivers.

I passed the environs of Trondheim, a bustling city pressed hard between where the River Nidelva meets the jagged Trondheim Fjord. Icy water was now running freely into every one of my gaping and extremely chilly orifices.

Whenever I closed the visor, the steam blinded me to the road. When I opened it a crack to clear it, a veritable wave of rainwater issued in to fill my eyes, ears, and mouth. I seemed to have put myself in the unlikely situation where I might soon become the only person to ever drown on a moving motorcycle.

I saw the sign for Trondheim city centre and slowed the bike to consider turning off and exploring.

Trondheim is famous for being the ancient city of the Vikings. The city was originally named *Kaupangen*, meaning trading place, by the Viking King Olav Tryggvason in the year 997 CE. Trondheim was the capital of Norway until 1217 and is still the third most populous municipality in the country.

I saw the city spread out below me from the high road above it. From that aspect, in the grey and the heavy rain, everything about the city looked commercial and busy. As pretty as the town might actually be in the sunshine, it held no appeal for me in that moment. I kept on riding.

The Viking's were amazing sailors, skilled navigators, and ruthless warriors. Infamous in Britain for their seamanship and plundering of the coastal towns, they also voyaged as far as the Mediterranean, North Africa, the Middle East, and North America, even discovering and settling Newfoundland.

There is an amazing true story about the Vikings arrival in ancient Byzantium, the city that is now modern Istanbul. Viking warriors journeyed south through Europe navigating the Seine, the Rhine and the Danube to finally sail down the Black Sea to reach Istanbul. When they got there, they were so feared and respected, the Emperor of Byzantium recruited them as bodyguards. In the service of their Byzantium rulers, these Viking warriors learned the nuances of the city and the secrets of the empire. But these warriors soon became bored with being employed as bodyguards and instead used the intimate knowledge of the city they had gained, to turn against their employers and laid siege to the city. They turned from protectors to marauders and sacked the great city and plundered it of its wealth.

The Vikings were much more than brutal pirates (although many believe the Old Norse for Viking literally meant Pirate Raid), they even established the Tynwald, the world's oldest continuous parliamentary body, on the Isle of Man, the island that sits in the middle of the Irish Sea off the western coast of England, and they gave English the core of its language, much of which is based on Old Norse. If you are a Jackson, Benson, Stevenson or Watson your lineage is likely to be Viking. Many of our words that relate to objects and actions such as skirt, cake, fog, freckles, neck, moss, sister, window, knife, smile, seat, gift, egg, cross, leg, steak and Thursday—named after Thor, are all derived directly from Old Norse.

The further north I rode, the rain only intensified further, the ice water continued to trickle down my neck and fill my over suit.

I began to slowly understand the Viking passion for invasion. It was clearly the appalling weather here that made them so angry, and willing to row thousands of miles across tempestuous oceans to deprive others in sunnier climbs of their comfort and possession. I could only assume Old Norse also gave us the words for rain, drip, shower, downpour, waterproof, umbrella, wellington and mackintosh, words handed down to us through the generations. But when I checked, and as much as I wanted it to be the case, that turned out to not be entirely accurate. Or, in fact, true in any way.

By the time I made it to Vegset I was as soaked through, shivering and miserable as it was possible to be. I found a campsite, jumped off the bike and bent down to unbutton the legs of my over suit and release the fifteen gallons of glacial downpour that had accumulated there. I had intended to pitch my tent once more, but when I checked the inside of my bags, they were soaked too, tent, clothes and, worse of all, my sleeping bag was like a huge quilted but drenched dishcloth.

Defeated for the day, I paid for a *Hytter*, an A-Frame timber hut that many of the larger campsites had available for those few individuals dumb and damp enough to arrive by motorcycle. It was small but cozy, warm and so heavily scented with the tree of its construction, it was like having sharp pine needles jammed into the smaller crevices of your nose. It was like being trapped inside a pine scented Glade air freshener. My personal sauna. I unpacked all of my soaked possessions and stretched them out across the small bed and hard wooden chair to dry.

I had some packets of dried soup in my panniers and having sickened myself of boiled eggs for the day, I re-hydrated one and heated it up over my little burner. With the scant nourishment and meagre vitamins derived from a meal of flecks of dried pea and carrot I called dinner complete. I played some *'Need you Tonight'* by INXS on my little Walkman and then, exhausted by the day, took myself off to my creaking pine scented bed.

Arctic Circle

In the morning, I carefully re-packed my sleeping bag and all of my clothes. They had dried out a little but were all still disturbingly cold and damp to the touch. It was slowly dawning on me that, for the duration of this trip, I was to remain perennially soggy. My fingertips and toes were as wrinkled as if I had taken a long bath.

With my little Hytter emptied of clothing I spread the map while I brewed some coffee. Outside my little window the sun was struggling to escape the dark embrace of a huddle of brooding clouds that swamped the horizon. Still, it was dry at the moment, and that would have to do.

The terrain was not being as conducive to fast mileage as I had planned when looking at the maps back in the UK. There were no motorways here, not even dual carriageways. That was a pleasant experience in many ways, and I was enjoying the riding, but it also meant that my calculations for expected daily mileage were still way off. Towns, river crossings, switchbacks and high mountain passes were taking much longer to navigate than I had anticipated or planned for, even after abandoning my original plan to explore the western islands on the way north.

My goal today was to ride to a campsite somewhere close to the town of Bodø, located only a few miles inside the Arctic Circle.

Inside the relative warmth and dryness of the Hytter, I pulled on a pair of wet underpants, donned some socks that actively dripped and created small puddles on the pine floor, struggled to pull on a pair of leather jeans over damp, clammy legs and manfully wrestled with a soaking wet t-shirt that clung to any part of my upper torso it touched.

Outside, with my things packed on the bike, I pulled on damp gloves and a moist helmet, zipped up my soggy leathers against the chill of the morning air and set off.

For the first part of the morning, the mountains were behind me. I was riding through a green, fir lined valley. It was almost redolent of the low Alpine hills in Austria, and I took the opportunity to let the bike stretch its legs while traffic was light, and the roads were relatively flat and straight. I barely saw another vehicle and the scenery was, for the most part, obscured by the tree line, it was like riding through a vast green tunnel, vision drawn to the infinity of the next bend.

I stopped to fill up the tank just outside a town called Mosjøen. The garage had a little Circle K type store next to it and I took the opportunity to simultaneously sell my soul to Lucifer and empty my bank account in order to buy more eggs, a sliver of ham and a pack of rustic, seed speckled buns. I even treated myself to a bottle of beer, paying close to five times what I would have paid back in the UK.

A little further up the road was a parking place by the side of the Vefsnfjord and I pulled over to eat my lunch. The water reflected the density of the sky. It was filled with clumps of cloud, they hung low and threatening in the sky like cabernet purple grapes on the vine, filled with the future promise of another drenching. Across the water, on the far side of the deep fjord lay a bulk of land the shape of a felled troll, it sprawled across the landscape, stripped bare of shrub and tree by the winds that drove in directly from the western seas. It was chilly here; I was beginning to feel the extremity of my northern latitude at last. I shivered in the dampness of my clothing and wondered if I would ever be warm again.

The road ran alongside one fjord or another for a hundred miles or more. It wasn't until I reached the town of Mo I Rana that the road veered inland and the terrain began to change once more. I began to climb, through one switchback, and then another, the bike pulled me up onto a lofty landscape that was almost lunar. Flat tundra stretched out before me. The mountains of the Saltfjellet–Svartisen National Park were distant; a snow peaked and jagged saw blade, a sharp edge across the horizon.

The land was barren and windy, swept clean of gorse, bracken, and even low-lying heather. Mosses and lichens clung low to the ancient bedrock, afraid to raise their heads too high into the meagre and rare blades of sunshine lest they be uprooted and swept away on gales that never faltered. Clouds, heavy with moisture and the promise of rain clung to low hills and dales. Only hardy Alpine Rock Cress and Catchfly, snow white and purple, dared peep their blooms above the permafrost crusted surface.

Graduated orange snow sticks were planted on either side of the road and, in the shaded lee of the gorse, lay drifts of snow, remnants of the last winter, or so I fervently hoped. The rain began to patter across and streak my visor and I let out a groan. I began to look for a place I could pull over and don my waterproofs when I passed a sign—*'2 km*

- Arctic Circle'. I had made much better time than I could have hoped for, and my heart surged with excitement.

Up ahead I saw a bunch of cars parked by the side of the road and just south of the line of latitude 66°34'N I parked the bike. I struggled into my red and black condom to protect against the now steady downpour and took a picture of me next to the bike with the sign for the Arctic Circle in the background. I remember clearly that the wind was howling with a wild fury, and I was hunched, tight against the cold as I set up my camera on a rickety fence post and set the timer, to run frantically back into shot before the shutter clicked.

The Arctic Circle marks the southernmost latitude where, on the day of the June solstice, the longest day of the year in the northern hemisphere, the sun will simply refuse to set. Correspondingly, on the December solstice, the shortest day of the year in the northern hemisphere, the sun will fail to rise. These phenomena are referred to as the midnight sun and the polar night respectively. My trip took place in July, and as I had slowly journeyed north the sun had set later and later and, despite the rain and heavy clouds, the nights had become brighter. At tonight's camp I expected to get my first view of the midnight sun.

Nothing marked the line of the Arctic Circle when I visited in 1989, just a sign, the blurred blue one behind me in the photo I took. There is a modern visitors centre there now with parking, toilets, a small restaurant, and the compulsory gift shop where you can buy miniature trolls with orange spiky hair and fluffy reindeers to take home to later lose or put straight in the trash, so I am glad I visited when I did. Although I have to admit, a flushing toilet and a warm hand dryer, followed by a hot reindeer burger and a cup of something that steamed would have been welcomed.

I stood for a full minute or so as the rain swept in, taking in my surroundings and marvelling that I was now actually inside the Arctic Circle and then, with that experience fully sampled I jumped back on the bike, popped a small wheelie across the famous line of latitude just because I figured not many people could claim they had crossed it on one wheel, and set off north towards the town of Saltstraumen where I planned to camp.

Saltstraumen was a little off course for me, but I had bumped into a couple of Dutch bikers at a petrol station, and they had recommended it to me. The name of Saltstraumen is derived from the region '*Salten*' and '*straumen*', which means stream, but the name doesn't do the phenomenon that can be seen there, true justice. The narrow straight under the elegant arch of the bridge that connects the outer Saltfjorden to the large Skjerstad Fjord between the islands of Straumøya and Knaplundsøya is two miles long but only five-hundred feet wide and when the tide turns, the Saltstraumen Maelstrom can be seen. It is one of the strongest tidal currents in the world, formed when over one hundred and ten billion gallons of water attempt to churn through the narrow gap, all at the same time. Vortices thirty feet across and sixteen feet deep swirl the depths into gigantic whirlpools.

I was fortunate to arrive just as the tides changed and it was worth the extra few miles. As the sea water began to surge through the narrow channel, the sound level began to increase, a turbulent hiss and rumble as the water was accelerated, it soon began to seethe and spin. In only a few seconds the flat of the fJord resembled the surface of a vast pan of violently boiling water. The deep blue of the sea became multi-hued, cobalt and arctic blue, flecked with bright green algae wrenched from the sea floor, all topped white with raging, swirling froth and foam. A long line of maelstroms formed on either side of the channel making the passage entirely unnavigable. I couldn't imagine what it would be like to be caught in such raw, elemental turbulence in a small boat in open water.

As the waters calmed, I got back bike on the bike. The rain continued to stream from the darkened heavens above. The road was slick. I wasn't sure if it was because

I was so far west, off the well beaten track perhaps, but for the first time, the roads were rough and patchy with broken concrete. I piled into a tight right-hander and was surprised to feel the bike squirm beneath me, the back wheel lost traction and started coming around to catch up the front wheel in a most unsettling manner. I counter steered to correct the slide and got around the bend OK, but my heart was beating hard, and for the rest of the day I backed off the throttle and navigated the tighter bends like a little old lady in furry boots walking to the post office on an icy road.

I got as far as Godøynes Camping. It was south of the town it was named for, on a long and bent index finger of a peninsula that jutted out like it was beckoning somebody from across the azure and perfectly still Skjerstad Fjord.

The day was long, and I was tired and wretchedly damp, but although several Hytters were advertised as available, I didn't have sufficient funds to afford one, so I pitched my tent in the sloping meadow beneath the lee of an over-hanging cliff that sheltered me a little from the cold rain.

I boiled an egg and ate the last of my ham on a bone-dry roll. I remembered the bottle of beer I had purchased and popped the cap and took a sip. It was as cold as I was from the long day's ride and I sipped it as I absent mindedly picked poppy seeds from between my teeth, all the while marvelling at a seagull grey sky that, even at eleven thirty at night, was daylight bright.

Bridges and Ferries

The next day I woke early. The sun had been streaming through the membrane of my little tent for much of the night. This was unusual but to be expected at this extreme latitude. What made it extraordinary was that it was the sun that was shining. The rain had finally stopped.

I poked my head outside to see the surface of the fjord sparkling, a million shards of glass twinkling, every facet a blinding glare. I got dressed, cringing at the touch of damp socks and a cold, clammy shirt, quickly checked the tire pressures and tension of the chain and gave the bike a general lube and polish. I was eager for the road, to make the best of this wonderful and unexpected change in the weather.

The proximity of the border with Sweden had pushed me back, close to the coast, and all of the "lovely crinkly edges" of the fjords, so adored by Slartibartfast. Today would be a day of S-bends, cutbacks, bridges and ferries as I carved my way across this glacier sculpted part of the world. The air carried the tang and chill of early Spring which was a bit of an annoyance on a motorcycle as it was actually the middle of Summer. But the sky was clear and as blue as a cornflower. The lakes and fjords perfectly mirrored the snow-capped peaks and forested glens.

The road was so contorted and twisted by the terrain that I could often see the road I would soon be travelling only a mile across the water from me. I would ride north for twenty minutes and then, frustratingly find myself on the other side of the fjord riding south again. But I was flying, the sun in my eyes, my shadow stretched and elongated, a constant companion. Past ice blue glacial lakes, over high mountain passes and through narrow damp and dripping tunnels that bore through the sides of granite peaks. I rode all day.

At Bognes I turned a tight corner and found that the road just ended in a large car park, and I was forced to take the ferry across the Tsfjorden to Skarberget.

It was lovely to park up the bike amidst the camper vans and cars and drink a coffee, coddled and steaming in cold hands. The surface was placid, and we slipped through the water with ease. Seabirds soared overhead, following us, thinking perhaps that we were a fishing smack and might soon give the promise of a free meal. Across the still water was a line of mountains, jagged and wind broken, a long line of tumbled tombstones.

The road became constrained by the shape of every fjord. At all times it ran close to the shore, faithfully following every bay and creek, inlet, and promontory. A continuously snaking, twisting, turning serpent. I moved my weight around the bike, leaning left and then right in an eternal dance, enjoying the rare sunshine and a bike that seemed to strain forward with the need to drive harder and harder into each new bend. The engine note was a low howl and the red needle on the tacho swung across with glee towards the red zone as I smiled inside my still damp helmet.

At lunchtime I followed the road up a series of switchbacks that drew me ever higher. The air chilled as I climbed until, around one final bend it brought me out into a land akin to the landscape I had seen close to the Arctic Circle on the previous days ride. All trees petered out to be replaced by hardy fern and bracken. The low and featureless hills ran into the distance for endless miles, the road a solitary dark grey ribbon. Mile after mile I rode across the tundra, seeing little traffic and no sign of civilization except the manmade tarmac beneath me.

Suddenly, in the midst of this wilderness, entirely incongruous in its surroundings, stood a small restaurant, entirely alone just off the road, surrounded by countless miles of more and more nothingness. Intrigued, I pulled the bike into the small and mostly deserted car park. I walked across the car park in my squelching, squeaking boots and slipped through the door to the restaurant so as to not let out too much heat.

I was worried about being able to afford anything the menu might offer, but I was desperately hungry for something that wasn't egg shaped. I took a seat by a long window that overlooked the vast but strangely beautiful emptiness, and the young waitress furnished me with a glossy laminated menu.

The waitress was dressed in a bright red and blue tunic with a fur collar and wore fur boots on her feet. I looked at my surroundings, bright wall coverings and reindeer antlers and I realized—slowly I admit, even for me—that I was in the land and the presence of the Sámi.

When I was younger, we called this area Lapland and its tribal people and culture Laplanders or even more ignorantly Eskimos. The Sámi prefer the name given in their own language. The Sámi largely ignore modern borders, they range across all of the northern latitudes of Norway, Sweden, Finland and the Murmansk Oblast region of Russia. They subsist through coastal fishing, fur trapping, and sheep herding, although their best-known means of livelihood is semi-nomadic reindeer herding.

The menu only had a few items listed, all reindeer based, but the prices were actually fairly reasonable, and the menu had helpful pictures of the food. One of the items within my price range was a Reindeer burger and, enormously intrigued, I ordered one and a large coffee. When it arrived, I took a huge and hungry bite. The flavour was similar to venison, as you would expect, gamey but extremely tender. I washed it down with the hot, black coffee and burped my approval just as the waitress came back.

"likte du det?" She asked.

I obviously don't speak Norwegian but, given the context of the situation, I was pretty sure that she was inquiring if I had enjoyed the meal. I nodded and smiled that I did.

"Ja. Ja." I said.

She tapped me on the shoulder and pointed out of the window.

"Boazu."

At first, I struggled to see what she was pointing at, so well matched were they by their native environment, but then I saw the movement and a flash of blue fabric. Two Sámi herdsmen. One tall, taking long strides across the tundra, the other shorter and struggling to match the man's pace. A man and a boy. Father and son perhaps, moving across the terrain. In front of them was a herd of around twenty to thirty reindeer.

The reindeer were much smaller than Santa had led me to believe. More like really large dogs, their heads came up to the level of the father's waist, although the antlers, gracefully arced and pointed, approached the level of the fur hat he wore on his head. The group all moved with practiced ease across the challenging terrain, man, and beast together in their timeless waltz. As we watched, they made their slow way across to us.

My waitress held her right hand to her heart as she continued to point and look out at the man and the boy.

"Min far, min bror," she said. My father, my brother.

I smiled and left as big a tip as I could afford, which believe me was not as much as it probably should have been. I thanked her and went outside to see them approach.

They were passing within a few feet of where I had parked my bike, so I sat on a low nearby wall, quietly so as not to spook the animals. The reindeer's coats were dark brown, eyes golden, set beneath the impressive curved 'C' of velvet coated antlers that curved backward along their heads. Their hooves were covered in soft fur, and they passed me with barely a sound, like a hushed and secretive whisper from a distant era. The father held up a hand as tough, wrinkled, and brown as a chestnut and I waved back with a hand soft and pale in comparison. It was a magical moment. A perfectly moving, breathing metaphor for that wild, merciless wilderness.

Back on the bike I made the most of a full stomach and a sun-kissed road. I was soon back in the mountains and making good progress north. I had decided to take another small diversion for no good reason other than the name intrigued me. I had decided to ride east a few tens of miles to stop just outside the city of Tromsø. I had heard of Tromsø of course. But I also knew, deep down, that there was something there that I had always wanted to see, although, for the life of me I couldn't recall what it was. But I trusted in my own fallible memory and took the chance.

I stumbled across the campsite in the early evening, the watery sun was still high in the sky. The campsite, on the outskirts of Tromsø was the largest and most organised I had seen on all of my travels and the price for the single nights camp didn't make my eyes water or completely empty my now moth filled wallet.

I quickly parked the bike and put up the tent for I had, for the first time on this trip, spotted an actual modern shower block.

I pretty much sprinted across to the shower block and immediately stripped out of all of my wet clothing. In my towel I had wrapped my driest pair of underpants, a pair of squelchy socks and a t-shirt. I hung them all on the drying line beneath a heating lamp and then jumped under the shower head to luxuriate for the best part of half-an-hour underneath the searing blast of hot water.

A hot steam engulfed me. My skin slowly turned a worrying hue of red. I cared not a jot. The hot water blistered the frighteningly pale skin on my chest, arms, and legs. I opened my mouth and let the water pour in to wash away the chills. I just let the piping hot water wash the aching cold from my bones until it hurt so much, I could stand it no longer. I was actually sweating when I finally turned off the shower head. Sweating and smiling and as happy as I had been in several days. Even the almost constant, rapid chattering of my teeth, the sound of which had become a constant and personal internal metronome, had somewhat abated.

I heard somebody in the stall next to mine shout something in Norwegian that sounded awfully close to, "what moron used all of the hot water," so I decided to retrieve my clothes from the line, get dressed and hit the town.

I won't lie. When I took them down from the drying line, my clothes, by any measure of normality were still incredibly damp. But they were dryer and warmer than anything I had worn since I got off the ferry in Bergen. With a veritable spring in my step and a whistle in my throat, I walked across the long Tromsø bridge to the island of Tromsøya where the city centre is located.

It was very beautiful, filled with old wooden houses, some dating back to 1789. They were all painted lively hues of blue and orange, set amidst gleaming fjords and towering snowy distant peaks, it was breath taking.

A brief warning, a heads up if you will allow. When you visit Tromsø you need to get used to hearing the word 'northernmost'. Tromsø is a city replete with the 'northernmost' of all things. The world's northernmost University, northernmost planetarium, northernmost botanical garden, northernmost tennis club, northernmost Premier League football club. Indeed, The Norse chieftain Ohthere, who lived in Tromsø during the 890s described himself as living "furthest to the North of all Norwegians" with areas north of this being populated only by the Sámi.

I had a walk around the northernmost part of the town to make sure I was the northernmost visitor in Tromsø, browsed inside some wildly expensive shops and feigned interest in some historical buildings that may or may not have been culturally meaningful (I had no tour guide and couldn't read the signs, they were all written in Norwegian when I visited in 1989, and the idea of a guided audio tour was many years away), and then I saw a sign that reminded me why I had heard of the city. It was a sign for the Tirpitz Memorial Museum.

When I was a kid I always quite fancied joining the Royal Navy, and warships and destroyers sparked a young fella's imagination. The Tirpitz had been Hitler's largest single weapon during World War II. The second of two Bismarck-Class Battleships built to help defeat Britain and Russia. She was stationed off Håkøy Island near Tromsø and for years she wreaked havoc on the Baltic and North Atlantic convoys supplying the Allies.

On the 12th of November 1944 it took thirty-two Lancaster bombers dropping twenty-nine tallboy bombs to destroy and sink her. She remains there today, at the bottom of the icy fjord that she once called her home.

Unfortunately, it was getting late, although the sun was still high above the jumbled roofs of the town. The museum was a good few miles away, too far for me to walk and

I could not afford a taxi. Back in the pretty town I found that, predictably, all of the bars and restaurants were far beyond my limited means, so, tired and famished I found a local grocery store on the edge of town, bought a pack of beers and some bread and walked back across the bridge to boil an egg or two for another lonely dinner.

Back at the tent I ate my sad meal. I checked my watch and was surprised to see that it was almost 10:30 at night. The sun was low across the cityscape, it seemed to skim above the roofs and chimney stacks of downtown Tromsø, but above me the sky above was a deep bright blue. A perfect summer's day in the middle of the night.

Portent of a Storm

The patter of rain on the tent woke me with a weary groan. I had enjoyed Norway in the sunshine, but it seemed that such a pleasure was a rare treat even in these summer months. At least one that had mostly been denied to this persistently moist and increasingly fungus-covered motorcyclist.

I had complicated matters for myself by stopping off to visit Tromsø. I now had to decide to either ride back the way I had come or to set off due north, which would be shorter from a pure mileage perspective, but would take more time as it required two ferry journeys. I decided on the ferry route simply because I do so enjoy a boat ride, and it would offer a bit more variety to the day.

I slipped on my waterproof over suit and walked around the site collecting all of my belongings and packing them on the bike. In my over suit I made a noise like somebody opening the world's biggest bag of crips every time I moved a limb, and I soon had the whole campsite awake and peering blearily out of tents to see what the commotion was. They would all soon find out that the same noisy bastard that woke them all up had also used all of the hot water in the showers too.

I packed the tent and made doubly certain that all of my clothes and sleeping bag were safely ensconced in the large yellow plastic bag that sported my employers big 'BT' logo and a picture of 'Buzby' the chatty animated bird from the adverts with Maureen Lipman that ran at the time in the UK. That was at a happy time in the company's history, when BT was a fun place to work, back when it was still trying to transform from a public company with a heart, to a privatized conglomerate intent only on the success of its shareholders—I would take voluntary redundancy soon after I returned from this trip.

My first ferry was at Breidvik, a tiny port nestled between a skyline dominated by a series of granite snow-capped humps. They looked all the world like the backs of a pod of giant killer whales, breaking free of the ocean, to hunt seal in the cold Arctic waters. The tide was out when I arrived and the beach that ran parallel to the approach road was exposed, a vast swathe of gold that stretched almost all the way across the estuary. Out at sea, a cold wind whipped the water into angry peaks and chilled the air, and I pulled my collar tighter under my chin as I waited for the ferry to board.

We boarded and I made sure the bike was safely on its centre stand and secured by tie-downs, and went to find a seat at the prow to relax, the onus of navigation and riding removed from me for a moment. I sat at the prow letting the cold wind of our progress push back my scant locks, drinking in the view of the distant mountains. I was lost in a little reverie of my own when the skipper poked his head out of the wheelhouse and shouted as he pointed to starboard.

"Se delfiner."

I looked to my right to see the rising dorsal fins and arched shining, almost rubber moulded backs of a pod of dolphins. There were seven or eight, swimming closely together they streaked through the water, one at a time they leaped from the fjord and crashed back in with a loud slap and a high plume of white flecked seawater.

"De jakter på makrell," the skipper shouted, which I could only assume meant that the Dolphins were seeking to catch mackerel in the icy depths of this majestic fjord.

It is amazing what you can pick up from a foreign tongue if you just choose to listen. If you open your mind to the possibility of understanding, it is possible to, almost osmosis like, to be able to find interpretation even in such a foreign tongue. It also helps, of course, if you are willing to just plain make shit up. He could have just as easily been saying, "The boat is sinking, swim for land you fool."

I think I might have been correct about the mackerel though because nobody jumped overboard. In fact, one of the other passengers, a Norwegian fellow, struck up a conversation with the captain. I could hear them, but the meaning of the rest of the conversation was beyond me and I returned my attention to the dolphins. I had never seen dolphins in the wild before and I was entranced. So agile and swift, they quickly outstripped the ponderous ferry. They would slip beneath the waves for several seconds, I had an idea, probably from watching too much David Attenborough, that they might be diving deep to drive fish back upwards towards the surface where they would be trapped and become easy prey.

For a full minute they disappeared completely, and I thought the spectacle had left us. And then one last surprise, they surfaced only inches from the hull of the boat, heading back the way we had come. They were so close, I could, for just a moment, see a clear glassy eye, full of wisdom, a glossy grey head, and a row of teeth. For one long moment they were next to me and then just as quickly they were gone.

We landed in the tiny town of Svensby twenty minutes later and then, less than a fifteen-minute ride around the headland, I found myself waiting for another ferry in Lyngseidet to make the forty-minute crossing to Olderdalen. Lyngseidet was a small town that lay in the lee of an impressive range of gigantic, towering peaks. The ferry was already boarding, just four or five other cars waited in the queue ahead of me.

This crossing was the first where I took notice of the weather. The wind had picked up considerably and the surface of the fjord was white peaked. The flat-bottomed ferry rolled and rose and fell over the waves in a slowly sickening motion.

I looked up to see the sky had filled with thick, black nimbostratus and the wind had changed direction. When I woke there had been a light breeze from the east. Now there was a stiff and icy wind from the west. For the first time on a ferry, I was happy to make landfall and reclaim control of my own destiny back on the motorcycle.

The ferry terminal at Olderdalen was small and isolated but the snow crowned mountains encroached close upon the road. It reminded me very much of the Cairngorms but on an even grander scale. I turned left at the T-junction, towards the town of Kirkenes, the road skirting the very edge of the vast Lyngen fjord for mile after mile.

I rode for most of the day as the weather around me continued to deteriorate. The road meandered its slow and gradual way, often twisting to the east and then taking a long loop south to navigate some gigantic inlet but then inexorably taking me back northward. The scenery everywhere was spectacular, but the wind had scrubbed the reflections of the mountains from the surface of the fjords.

In the late afternoon, I crossed a little bridge north of Sørstraumen. It whisked me across a bay whipped into frenzied motion by the wind. The view of the distant snow-covered hills beneath a sky blown into fast streaming motion was so spectacular that I pulled over by the side of the road and just stared to let the image sink into my memories.

I looked at my watch. I had been riding for over six hours and had covered less than one hundred and twenty miles. The ferries alone had accounted for ninety minutes of just waiting and subsequent slow travel. I was beat. Too tired to continue. I had hoped to make it to Nordkapp by evening, but I was still the better part of a day away and the weather was still closing in.

I turned the bike around and re-crossed the bridge. I had seen signs for a small and very rural campsite just before I had crossed and for today it would just have to suffice.

To Nordkapp

S leep had been elusive. All night long the wind had rattled and shaken the tent. I had worried that the constant snaps of the fabric might tear the tent or lift the tent pegs. The night had been darkened by the heavy clouds, but raven blackness had never truly fallen.

I rolled out of my sleeping bag and pulled myself awkwardly into clothes. Today would be a good day. By evening I would be pitching my tent at the very northern tip of Europe. Tonight, I would be at North Cape.

The morning started dry although heavy banks of clouds piled on the horizon ready to be flung by the never-ending gusts of wind across the sky.

The morning took me north along the banks of countless fjords, the usual mirrors of the mountains fractured by the rising peaks of the frigid water. Low hills lay scattered across the landscape. Stunted trees lay across granite outcrops like a three-day stubble on an old man. The miles drifted by. Not always north. Often the road swopped south to avoid the intrusion of a fjord or the crack of a mountain.

The weather continued to close in, and now the rain came in starts and stops. The road was slick and slippery, I was chilled but still filled with optimism and excitement. Sometime around mid-morning, close to the town of Alta I saw a single red and white striped motorcycle parked by the side of the road. It was piled high with luggage, tent and sleeping bags. There were few vehicles this far north and almost no bikes, so it was unusual enough to catch my attention. A man and a woman, he in black and silver waterproofs and she in bright orange, were sat on a nearby Armco barrier by the side of a heaving fjord, eating a sandwich and smoking a shared cigarette. The sound of my bike caught their attention and they both looked up together to smile and wave to me as I passed by. I nodded and gave them a little salute with my clutch hand as I passed.

Forty miles up the road when I had stopped for a bite to eat and have a quick pee behind a bush, they overtook me, and we exchanged waves again. This repeated itself as the day unfolded. We were travelling at about the same pace and clearly towards the same destination, so the next time I saw them, instead of waving and passing, I pulled over.

Their names were Georgie and Ella. Both German, both from somewhere close to Dusseldorf. They spoke sufficient English for us to quickly become friends. He had the look of the Teutonic about him, very tall with broad shoulders, short cropped blond hair and blue eyes in a surprisingly square head. Ella was tall with long raven hair and coffee-coloured eyes. Georgie was a huge guy who really needed a bigger bike. He rode it like Donkey Kong in Mario Kart with poor Ella squashed onto the pillion amongst the jumbled luggage.

Unlike the wealthy and well kitted out Germans I met in southern Europe in the prequel to this story, Georgie and Ella were of the budget biker variety, much like myself. They were riding a tatty and older model Kawasaki Z500 and sported a mis-matched hodge-podge of scratched and patched leathers and weatherproof gear of dubious provenance and equally doubtful water resistance. They were my kind of people, and upon confirming my suspicion that they too were bound for North Cape, we shook hands with a smile and resolved to ride the rest of the way together.

We rode through the worsening conditions for the remainder of the day, stopping every now and again to stretch cramped legs and share a bite to eat, they providing ham and mustard sandwiches and me supplying the obligatory and unavoidable boiled eggs. The wind had continued to pick up and now it drove in with a fierce high-pitched wail across the tundra. At the same time, it drove a blanket of frigid rain and the occasional pelt and sting of hail to lash us, a storm front from the west, bringing icy conditions directly from the Norwegian Sea only a few miles over the headland.

Despite our increasing journey northward the light had continued to leach from the sky. The clouds had thickened, pushed by the low pressure to pile up high above us. A swiftly moving lower layer of cloud streamed only feet above the touch of our helmets. It carried moisture and cold air, sleet, and strong sudden gusts that de-stabilized the airstream and the bikes.

The mountains had slipped behind us as we had climbed steadily onto a desolate and winds-stricken tundra. The gale plucked at us and sent the bikes to swerve dangerously across the road. We got some scant relief as we dropped down to skirt the massive, dark grey and heaving expanse of the Porsangerfjorden fjord, the land on the other side so distant it appeared like a low smudged finger of cloud on the distant horizon. The fjord lay to our right. To our left, almost within touching distance, ran a sheer cliff of crumbled stone that sheltered us, for a while at least, from the worst of the ravages of the storm.

I led the way, checking in my rear-view mirrors now and again that Georgie and Ella were keeping up. The surface of the Porsangerfjorden became more and more wind whipped and we could see real waves being peaked into white tipped breakers far from shore. The fjord had also continued to broaden as we rode north, closer to the place where it would finally issue into the Barents Sea, and the land on the far side had long since tipped over, to disappear behind the darkened horizon.

We rounded a left-hand bend that took us away from the fjord. The climb brought us out of the shelter of the cliffs. Suddenly we were exposed to the full brunt of the storm. Rain was flung horizontally across the road and the bikes were rocked and thrown by the gale force of the wind. I was forced to lean the bike hard to the left to fight the sudden gusts and to stay on the road. I looked in my mirror and could see Georgie having to do the same to stay in control.

Time and again the wind caught us and swept us across the road. A squall swept around us, unsettled the bikes and threw us heavily from side to side. The rain became a drenching driving blanket of misery. The road ahead disappeared into the veil of sweeping grey water, reduced our world to a fifty-yard rainwater filled window. Water pooled on my visor turning the world into a dappled and distorted blur. As soon as I wiped the excess water away with a damp glove it was instantly replaced a hundred-fold. The cold air caused my visor to fog, and I had to open it a crack to dispel the moisture. I slammed it shut again immediately as the rain and hail swept in to sting lips and bite cheeks.

Nordkapp, North Cape itself, is situated on the very northern tip of the island of Magerøya that sits alone in the stormy Barents Sea at the very top of the world. If you travel to North Cape by road today, you will be whisked across the three miles that separates the island from the mainland by a tunnel built in 1999. Back in 1989, when I travelled, there was a large ferry and a small terminal building and it was with some relief that I finally pulled the bike into the parking lot beside the terminal and saw out of the corner of my visor, Georgie do the same thing. I looked across at him and killed the engine of my bike and lifted my visor.

I had to shout across the howl of the wind that plucked and snapped at the seams of my over suit. Even in the comparative shelter of the terminal building, both feet on the ground, the gale continued to rock the bikes.

"Are you guys, OK?"

He looked back across at me and shook his big head.

"That last part of that ride was fucking crazy man."

THE STORM

We were the only two bikes waiting for the ferry. Ten or eleven cars were also parked around us. We parked the bikes as close to the scant shelter that the terminal building provided and still buffeted and drenched by the rain, we ran the short way to the steps as the wind chased us. With a clanging door, we entered the waiting room of the terminal building.

In the waiting room there was a buzz of conversation, a comingling of foreign voices talking in hushed tones about the weather and the conditions, and when the ferry would arrive, and was anybody crazy enough to actually get on it.

I stood silently with Georgie and Ella looking out of the long window that faced the broad strait. The sea was a surging, black and bucking stallion of wind whipped peaks and white sea spray. Visibility was down to only a few hundred yards; a vast curtain of rain obscured any sight of the island of Magerøya, or even the incoming ferry.

I had never seen an ocean like it, except in episodes of '*when good cruises go bad,*' and '*Disaster – Lost at Sea.*'

"Are we going to keep going?" I asked.

Georgie was quiet for a few minutes while he thought about the options and took in the tempest taking place outside the shelter of the window.

"There is nowhere to stay here," he said simply. "No hotels, no camping places. I don't want to turn back."

Of course, he was right. Unless the ferry operator let us stay in the waiting room, which was extremely unlikely, we either continued on in the hope that there would be some better option at North Cape itself or give up and ride back south. But the nearest town of any description in that direction was over sixty wind exposed miles away. From where the ferry would land us, North Cape was less than a twenty-mile ride.

"Yeah. Let's keep going. There will be something at Nordkapp."

As we spoke, we heard the murmur of voices rise. The ferry was approaching.

Out of the shroud, cutting through the gloom that sought to envelop her, came the bright yellow painted prow of the ferry. We were all relieved to see that, despite the brutal gusts from the west, she appeared not to roll or pitch too badly, and she crested and cut through each surging wave with stability and panache. She had been born for these waters and conditions.

It was still July after all, although it was difficult for us who hailed from more southern climbs to envision conditions worse than these, the winters here surely brought them. She had a deep draft and watertight compartments, a pointed steel and reinforced prow for breaking ice and powerful engines. You could sail all the way across the North Atlantic in winter in a ship like that.

The ferry docked with a roar of her engines and a blare of her horn, and we all began to prepare. The car drivers pulled up collars, dipped into pockets for keys and made a dash for the warmth and security of their cages and we three pulled on damp helmets and cold gloves and with a nod of reassurance at each other, like soldiers resigned to join an unwinnable battle, we walked across to the bikes and fired up the engines and cogged them into gear ready to join the ferry that was already busily disembarking.

The crew waved us on first and we parked close to the prow, pulling the heavy bikes onto centre stands for safety and stability. A crew member walked over and slung a ratchet tie down across both bikes and secured them tightly to anchors welded to the deck. He checked the straps by pulling on them and then muttered something unintelligible in Norwegian and holding up a thumb of reassurance.

The deck was cold iron, sea slicked and slippery. While the car drivers remained in their cars, we climbed up a set of steep iron grill steps onto an observation deck to crane our necks in an attempt to get a first view of our long anticipated final destination.

As the ferry set off, the wind was gusting, cold and wet onto her port side, so we three slipped around a bulkhead to seek shelter. On the starboard side it was relatively calm although we could all hear the screech of the wind as it broke itself in its fury on the hard angled steel of the ship. As the ferry drove forward and lines were slipped, the ferry sounded her klaxon once more. Clear of the harbour break water we could hear the pilot engage the ship's engines. A throaty roar sent a sheet of frenzied seawater high into the air and the ferry pulled herself forward with keen resolve through the heavy seas. Waves broke across her bows, and she surged up and over the crests and down into the valleys between, sending a salty, face reddening spray into our upturned faces.

Rain continued to sweep in from the west from weighted clouds, black and low across the sky. The floor of the ferry bucked and rose and fell and canted left and right under our feet. We all held onto a salt encrusted and seawater slick cold steel rail, knees bent against the endless swell.

I am not usually prone to sea sickness, but as the prow rose and fell and the ship rocked continually from side to side, I found my bile rising. I swallowed heavily and tried to focus on the horizon that was being thrown around the skies like a careless child flying a kite. For one long moment I was certain I was about to vomit and looked in a panic for the best place to lose the contents of my stomach. But then the extreme motion of the ship dislodged an eggy burp from down below and with that pressure released my stomach finally settled.

We could hear seabirds crying, and now and again one would be swept from the low clouds, a white herald of nearby land, sent by the wind to whip across our bows, only to rise again on frenzied wings and disappear into the clouds that threatened to touch the heaving seas. The gale brought with it a biting, bitterly cold blast of frigid air, and the dampness of our clothing let the freeze seep into our bones. We all stood shivering, eyes scanning the darkness ahead for a sign of land.

An apparition gradually appeared in the distance, and we screwed our eyes against the wind and the concealing veil of rain. The shoulders of the headland slowly revealed itself like the grim and ghostly spectre of death, shrugging off the concealment of its ghostly shroud. A lofty, brooding naked cliff face began to tower over us, and beneath, a squat concrete structure with the single gleam of a light, diffused and blinking through the driving icy rain. The promise of safety. The terminal building and dockside of the small town of Kåfjord.

Closer to the shore the ship's master had to fight the swells that sought to alternately sweep him onto the jagged, piercing rocks and then push him back, far out to sea. The engines roared, rising even over the angry pitch of the relentless wind. The ship rose and fell on thirty-foot swells. Slowly we closed the distance, a meter at a time we made slow but steady and reassuring progress. We must have passed a breakwater of some sort, although I did not see it in the persistent gloom of the day, but suddenly the ship settled. The captain sent the throttles forward and we coasted into the lee of whatever calmed the melee of the open sea.

With another surge of her engines the pilot brought the ferry tight alongside the dock. Heavy hawsers were flung from practiced hands to secure the boat, restore her bond to the land. The ferry boarding doors were winched down with a rhythmic clang, clang, clang, revealing to us, for the first time, the land of the island of Magerøya, and the dark ribbon of the northernmost stretch of public road in the world that would lead us across the island to our final destination. Nordkapp.

We rode the bikes carefully down the slippery ramp and off the ferry. Georgie took lead. We no longer needed a map, there was only the one road to follow.

The landscape was a desolate treeless tundra. Low hills surrounded the solitary strip of tarmac that pulled us northwards. Bubbling, churning rills and gullies criss-crossed the barren landscape. Vegetation, verdant scrub, and ochre leaved bracken clung low to the hills. Deep rifts had been driven through the crumbling bedrock by the relentless frost and thaw, crack, and splinter, of a thousand millennia. Icy pools lay scattered, held in frozen stasis by the permafrost of their surroundings.

Free of the shelter of the harbour I followed the dayglow orange back of Ella's waterproof. The rain came in a slew, a soaking deluge driven horizontally by the frenzied blast of the storm. As we climbed higher the winds came in irregular gusts and I watched as Georgie struggled to keep his bike on the road. Time and again a powerful and sustained howl of wind tore across the road forcing him to lean hard into its clutch, sending him reeling towards the crumbling and treacherous gravel broken edge of the road. As the gust suddenly and unexpectedly relented he was sent back reeling across the centre white line to the other side of the road. I was faring no better, in fact what was happening to Georgie was happening to me, only delayed by a second or more.

As we crossed this forbidding landscape and travelled ever higher and northward, each icy ferocious blast seemed to double in its intensity. The wind splintered itself in a sustained banshee wail around the edges of my rain drenched and fogging visor, plucked at my waterproofs and buffeted my helmet, making my head rock backwards and forwards, forcing me to clench my teeth in a grimace of concentration. Tension drained me, white knuckled I clung onto the handlebars, leaning the bike far over to my left to maintain contact with the road.

And then the inevitable happened. I saw Georgie blown hard across to the right-hand edge of the tarmac. He leant hard over to his left like a motorcycle racer in a tight hairpin, and I saw small stones flung into the air as his rear tire touched the gravel.

The wind was elemental in nature, I knew that intellectually. But still, it seemed to have an almost wicked intelligence. Like it was toying with us. Testing out abilities in this one-sided tug of war.

As Georgie managed to barely correct and recover from the fierce and seemingly unrelenting force from his left, the wind suddenly released him. He righted the bike as quickly as he could, and just as his momentum took him hard across to the other side of the road, a blast like no other came screaming across the open tundra from our left, blown in a fury straight from the exposed Barents Sea. It snatched him so suddenly and with such force he had no time to react. I watched in horror as he was swept back across the road and straight off the edge and into the furrowed and pitted, rock and tussock scattered land to our right.

I let out a low, "oh shiiiiit," even as I watched him go. And then the same sudden wind snared and caught me. I leant hard over in anticipation, but the power and intensity of the wind was relentless and could not be denied. I was swept across and over the edge of the road to join Georgia and Ella.

I remember bouncing hard over the first of the rocks and the gullies. The bike made a sickening crashing sound as the fairing grounded out on a hillock.

Out of the corner of my eye I could still see Georgie fighting to keep his bike upright, bouncing high and then crashing into clefts in the landscape, the bright orange blur of Ella's waterproofs, a single bright spot against the murky backdrop, rapidly disappearing into the darkness.

Whether Georgie was brave or stupid to continue to fight his fate, I couldn't tell. I quickly decided that this was a battle already lost. I closed the throttle and dumped the big Kawasaki under me and rolled clear. I was sent sprawling through puddles and across lumps of hard earth and grass, seeing a low darkened sky, tussocks of grass, sky, and then, finally, grass and oozing mud pressed hard against my visor.

I was winded and my side hurt. Panting hard I pushed myself to my knees and muttered to myself, "land of the fucking midnight sun my hairy biker's arse."

A Place to Stay

The four or five strangers, all dressed in just t-shirts and jeans and training shoes were soaked to the skin and now covered in mud and grass. Together we all managed to get my Kawasaki upright and we pushed it awkwardly and heavily back to the side of the road. It took several sweating and panting minutes. Some of the gullies were deep and footing was treacherous.

With my bike safe and upright, I looked back across the tundra and then started walking back to where I had last seen Georgie and Ella bouncing uncontrollably away. For a while, as I stepped through muddied puddles, up small stone strewn hillocks and across pebble filled brooks, I despaired. There was no sign of them. And then I came across a piece of amber coloured broken indicator lens.

"Georgie! Ella!" I screamed; my mouth cupped by frozen hands to make myself heard above the tortured scream of the wind.

The gale tore my words away in a ferocious and contemptuous howl. I walked on, staggering against the wind and the terrain. The gale snapped the fabric of my waterproofs, gunshot crack loud, as I began to despair. Then I saw it. A gleam of orange against the bleakness of this wilderness. Ella was climbing with difficulty to her feet, less than thirty yards away. I screwed my eyes and tried as best as I could to pick up my pace, terrified she was badly hurt. There was still no sign of Georgie. I staggered over hillocks, splashed through frigid puddles, breaking ice and slipping in gelid mud as I made my awkward way across the tundra. It was then that I saw Georgie. He had been there all the time, but in his black and silver one piece and black helmet, he had been invisible.

I rushed over and found them huddled over their bike. It was scratched and dented but mostly in one piece. But their sleeping bags had gone, caught by the wind and thrown far across the landscape, they were probably in Moscow by now being picked up by a confused commissar in Red Square.

I held Ella by the shoulders and shouted, "are you ok?"

She was ashen, with eyes wide, but she nodded, so I turned to Georgie to check he was ok. He was already trying to get his bike out of the small creek into which it had finally crashed.

I helped Georgie right the bike and I turned when I heard a shout to find a couple of my hardier rescuers, who had decided they would like to test their limits of endurance, while seeing if it was possible to get any wetter or muddier, had followed me to see if they could help some more.

"Come on," I shouted to Georgie over the wind.

"I need to find our sleeping bags," shouted Georgie, his hands cupping the words from his mouth so that I could catch them over the fury of the storm.

He started to walk away in the direction the wind would have taken them, hoping perhaps they had snagged on a rare branch or jagged rock. I followed him three or four paces and then saw him stop. I walked up behind him and sucked in a shocked breath.

Georgie had stopped on the very edge of a precipitous cliff that fell a sheer six hundred deadly feet into the black and angry breaking sea below us. Small pebbles broke away at our cringing toes to rattle and fall spectacularly down towards the waiting clutch of the breaking, jagged rocks and the angry seethe of the sea.

We both took two rather large steps backwards, even as the gale shoved us from behind, its final chance to seize and destroy us. We each swore in our native tongues. If Georgie had fought gravity and the inevitability of his crash for only a few seconds more, he and Ella would have plummeted, bike and all, down onto the sea splintered boulders far beneath us.

With a gargantuan effort we managed to wheel, lift, and cajole the bike back across the treacherous landscape and back to the road. The winds hadn't moderated at all. If anything, they were more sustained and savage. I shouted thanks to our rescuers, raising my voice over the shrill scream of the wind breaking over the edges of the rocks. We were all fatigued, puffing and panting, soaked to the skin and mud soiled. The drivers offered to form a protective convoy with their cars to keep us sheltered from the worst ravages of the storm. So, with only a few miles left to go we reluctantly got back on the bikes.

My Kawasaki started first time, but Georgie's had flooded, and we had to wait a few minutes for the carburettors to drain. We finally got both bikes running and nodded to the drivers of the cars who had waited for us. They drove on the wrong side of the road alongside us so that we rode in the lee of the meagre shelter they provided. Even with those barriers and protection the wind still buffeted us, and progress was slow.

By now the gale was so intense and the sheets of rain so dense, visibility was drawn down to a darkened landscape barely fifty feet across. All I could see was the outline of the black Saab to my left and a world rendered nebulous and nightmarish by the shroud of clouds that tore across the sky above my head. All I could hear, even through the insulation of my full-face helmet, was a high-pitched deafening howl.

Mile after slow and torturous mile we wended our way across the island. Drenched and cold, the adrenalin left me shivering, staring through a fog misted visor to pick out where the road went next.

Finally, with a huge sigh of relief I saw a sign for the visitor's centre. The road broadened into a large, paved car park and the three cars that had accompanied us tooted their horns and peeled away. We parked the bikes on the eastern side of the visitor's centre and walked inside. The automatic doors shut behind us with a hiss and we were suddenly deafened and disorientated by the instantaneous silence and lack of wind.

I took a quick moment to take stock of my physical condition and that of Georgie and Ella. I was breathing hard and with every breath in I winced, but I was pretty sure I hadn't broken a rib. My right shoulder hurt and when I glanced down, I saw a long tear in both my waterproofs and my trusty leather jacket where the arm met the shoulder. There was some gorse still sticking out of the flap. I couldn't have been more covered in mud if I had followed the hippos for a wallow down in the hollow.

My waterproofs were filthy, and my boots were wet and coated with an inch of black peaty soil. My helmet looked like it had been dragged through a ditch, which of course it had. Georgie and Ella were no better and we must have cut an unpromising trio. Georgie looked cold and pale but managed a smile as he thumped me on the shoulder, "man, what a fucking riot eh?"

Ella looked like she might cry.

There was a guard or custodian type official seated at a low desk just inside the second set of doors of the visitor centre. We stood panting for a second in the welcome shelter of the lobby before we stepped through the next set of doors to meet him. Inside it was a warm respite from the harsh conditions outside. It was snug and dry with electric lights, toilets, and a gift shop, but unfortunately our official was not so welcoming.

"You cannot come in here like that."

"What do you mean. It's a visitor's centre. We are visitors. And anyway, we need to shelter from the storm," I said.

"Not here. We are closing in ten minutes."

"But where are we supposed to go," asked Georgie.

"You will have to camp or go back to the mainland."

I laughed in exasperation, and I thought I heard Ella let out a ragged, high-pitched desperate sob, but that may have been me as well.

"We can't pitch a tent in this wind and we just both crashed in the storm. We can't go back tonight. We were hoping to shelter, to sleep here. Just on the floor or something, anywhere will do."

"Sorry but there is no way you are coming in."

He was maddeningly polite but adamant. I thought for a moment Georgie might pick him up and throw him over the nearby cliff. I saw the guard glance at Georgie's glowering expression and impressive bulk, and he decided to quickly close early. Pushing his advantage, he ushered us quickly outside and locked the door behind us.

"Now what," asked Ella.

We looked around us. There was absolutely nothing there. No hostel, no housing, nothing. And if it was even possible, the weather was deteriorating. Here at Nordkapp itself we were one-thousand feet high on a perfectly flat plateau, at the northernmost part of Europe at an impressively giddy latitude of 71°10′21″N. The next point of call was the Arctic ice sheets and then the north pole itself, which lay only a hop and a skip of 1,300 miles away. We were what you might say, a little exposed, and I strongly suspected our tents would not survive being erected never mind a night of this maelstrom.

"What is that over there? Asked Georgie, pointing back down the approach road and across the empty car park.

Visibility was dreadful, but through the gloom it looked like some construction was taking place. There was the silhouette of a green bulldozer and some pallets piled high with a blue tarpaulin snapping wildly in the wind. Next to that, looming out of the veil of the driving rain was a massive, long container, bright yellow and solid steel, like the ones you see being transported on container ships.

"Let's go see." I said.

Wearily, we got back on the bikes and made our way cautiously across the car park, buffeted and rocked continuously by the gale. We carefully parked the bikes in the shelter of the container and dismounted. I walked up to the double door of the container, Georgie at my side. The door was seven feet tall and fastened to the container by two sets of bulky hinges. I pulled the lever expecting it to be locked, but to our surprise it swung wide open with a shriek of tortured and unoiled steel.

In the back were seven motorcycles, and seated on multi-coloured blankets and sleeping bags in front of them, hands held outstretched around a small camping stove burning with a pale blue flame were seven German bikers.

"*Schließt die verdammt Tür, ihr verdammt wichsen,*" they all shouted as the wind and rain blew past me.

"What did they say," I asked turning to Georgie.

"They called you a fucking jerk off and told you to shut the fucking door," answered Georgie with a huge smile.

A Night Was Passed

The three of us quickly stepped inside and pulled the heavy door closed behind us with a clang. Georgie helped make the introductions while I looked around. My memory for names is poor even under the best of conditions, but I recall there was a Stefan and a Carl, a Tobias and maybe a Hannah or two.

There was something about bikers who were willing and able to make the journey this far north. Unlike the classy, well-equipped bikers I usually encountered in southern Europe, tall blond and well-groomed with matching leathers, expensive BMWs and hard luggage, this crowd looked positively feral.

The bikes were all rugged trail bikes, muddied and beat up. The luggage resembled that of my own and Georgie and Ella's, ragged tents and sleeping bags rolled into tatty plastic bags. The bikers were all thin and hungry looking, some had shaved heads and tattoos, some had long ragged greasy hair, they were all unkempt with hard darting gazes. I began to wonder if they might just kill us for sport and eat our faces.

It turned out they had good reason for their desperate expressions. They had arrived at Nordkapp just as the storm had swept in from the west and had all been sheltering together in this frigid shipping container for four long days with a dwindling supply of provisions.

The obnoxious guard at the visitor centre had grudgingly let them use the bathrooms, albeit one at a time, so they had access to water and bathrooms. But otherwise, they had been locked down by the weather. Hungry, cold and slowly rendered stir crazy by the sound of the howling, relentless gale, the cold four walls of the container and the monotony of their own company.

That was the trouble with making such a journey back in the days before the arrival of smartphones and the internet. Nowadays you would have been continually checking the conditions on your smartphone as you travelled north. Today's weather, the weekly forecast, temperatures, sailing conditions, availability of campsites and opening times. They would have all been constantly at your fingertips, allowing you to modify the journey as needed. You would have set off each morning informed and certain of how your day would unfold.

In fact, you would have already read the reviews from your armchair in the warmth of your home and decided to go to Disneyland instead. '*Nordkapp—one star, what a windy shit hole*'.

Not one person stranded in the container had even been given the opportunity to see what we all rode all of these thousands of miles to see, the view of the cliffs and the spectacular one-thousand-foot drop into the Barents Sea, all revealed under the spooky glow of the midnight sun. Everything had all been obscured by rain and cloud since they arrived.

With introductions made, me and Georgie slipped out of the door and back into the storm to retrieve our bags. The bikes were safe where we had parked them, and I took a minute to check for damage. There was a crack to the bottom of the fairing where I had bottomed out when I first left the road, and one of the indicator stalks had disappeared entirely, just the red and black wires hung from the casing, forlornly flapping in the wind. It was a miracle really, and although I was pissed about the crash and the damage it could have really been much, much worse.

Back in the container the Germans were still looking at us with hard flinty eyes. For some reason they seemed suspicious and reluctant to welcome us among them. I rifled through my panniers and pulled out what remained of the pack of beers, bread and cheese I had bought in Tromsø. Any remaining reticence from our new friends was instantly dispelled and we were all pulled by hungry arms into the circle with pats on the back and shouts of "willkommen, willkommen."

The feral Germans fell on the bread and cheese like a pack of hyenas on a limping rabbit, or a chubby American at a CiCi's pizza buffet. The carton of eggs I had bought in Tromsø had been flattened in the crash, but I pulled out my billycan and poured the eggy mixture into the bottom, bits of shell amongst them, to make a gritty omelette over the German's camping stove. When cooked we passed the billycan around, each taking a small share of the omelette and then picking egg shell out of our teeth as we ate.

The only light in the container was the flicker of the gas stove. It cast a blueish pool of light that reached only four or five feet. Anything beyond was cold midnight. Every now and again a shadowed and silhouetted face loomed suddenly out of the darkness to speak. Voices needed to be raised over the constant shriek of the wind beyond the steel walls of our little shelter.

Language was a barrier at first, but most of the Germans spoke a little English and Georgie was a patient interpreter. We discussed our travels. We drew maps with a stick in the dirt at our feet to show each other the routes we had individually taken to arrive at our little container located at the very end of the world.

I passed the beers, naturally chilled by the frigid air, around and received several hearty slaps on the back. In response, Georgie pulled out a half-drunk bottle of schnapps from his panniers and a loud and raucous cheer broke out. As the bottle was passed, we all began to share stories of our journeys and told jokes.

Laughter started to ring out around the circle. Toasts were made. Tobias stood, already a little tipsy. He gave me an English army salute and raised a toast to my English Queen. I raised an injured right arm of acknowledgment, intending to mirror his salute, but found that I couldn't easily bend my bruised elbow. I immediately realised I had entered into Basil Fawlty, 'don't mention the war,' territory with my unintended Sieg Heil. I groaned inwardly realising my Faux Pax, but everybody else thought it hilarious. Sounds of slightly stir crazy hilarity echoed around the container. One of the Hannah's was doubled up and cried out in German. I looked across to Georgie for translation. He stopped for a moment in his own laughter to help me.

"She says, she might have pissed herself and give the English asshole another drink."

Slowly, the few cans and the schnapps disappeared, and the container quieted down. Sleeping bags began to be pulled up tight under necks and bodies curled up to each other for warmth.

Despite their resemblance to a destitute and already heroin addicted thrash metal group, now fallen on even harder times, the group of seven was actually two different groups of friends thrown together by poor timing and happenstance.

Now we were ten, and the body heat of so many bodies slowly warmed the container nicely, although Yankee candle are unlikely to ever create a fragrance to match the perfume of that now cramped space, a heady mix of two-stroke oil, farts, leather, and the stench of too many unwashed armpits and feet.

With the food, the beer, and the schnapps consumed we all began to settle down for the night. I had no idea what time it was and when I nipped outside for a last pee it was the same dark racing sky and sweeping torrential rain as when we arrived. With the Germans locked down here for four days already I was beginning to really worry how long we would have to stay here before the weather released us.

In the morning, I woke with a groan. The steel floor had cramped my back despite the sleeping bag and loan of a blanket. It had been a rough night; the combination of the stench of so many stinking bodies and the interminable night-time honks, rasps and sqoink noises made the experience like trying to sleep on a hog farm. And that was just from where Georgie was sleeping.

Somehow the others around me were all still sleeping. The sound of their heavy breathing and wide mouth snoring, was buzz saw loud in the enclosed space. I pulled on my boots and shrugged into my leather jacket and as quietly as I could I slipped outside.

I was startled by the sudden flash of sunshine and had to raise an arm to shield my eyes as I quickly pulled the container door closed behind me. The day was bright and dry. The air fresh and chilled with the sharp acrid tang of the sea. A stiff wind still blew in from the west, but on the horizon was stretched out a line of pink duvet clouds.

During the night the storm had slipped us by. I walked over to the visitor centre, and, in the bathrooms, I spent a good ten minutes splashing cold water onto my face. I stripped off my leather jacket and the still wet t-shirt and raised an arm to reveal a bruise uncannily shaped like The Isle of Man, a blackened, purple still spreading welt, across the right side of my ribs that reached up and under my armpit. My right shoulder sported a nasty graze. Small, raised points of blood leached across the top of the shoulder and down the back of my arm. More worryingly, the joint was stiff and weak. I could barely raise the arm level with my own head without wincing and hopping around the bathroom for thirty seconds or so until the pain subsided.

I cleaned up as much as I could with some water and paper towels, used the bathroom and pulled my shirt and leather jacket back on. From the gift shop I bought a penny sized Nordkapp sticker for my helmet.

Outside was the famous Globe, a large wrought iron structure that has become the symbol for the site. I walked across to the edge of the cliff and peered down at the one-thousand-foot, sheer drop into the Barents Sea. I really wanted to be moved by the moment. It had been a long ride, and I still had a long way to go to get back home but, honestly, after the crash and the drama of the previous day I had entirely lost heart with the whole experience.

I only took a single photograph with my trusty Nikon, one of the iron Globe. My spirits were as low as a taint on a snake. I was aching and I was worried if there had been any less obvious damage to my precious Kawasaki. I wasn't as worried about myself as I was about the bike. Flesh is free as they say. I would heal up just fine. But this was in the days before foreign roadside recovery. To my knowledge anyway. Even if it existed, I certainly hadn't taken any out. If the bike broke down on my way back home, I had no means to get it back to the UK.

I took a second to look once more over the edge of the cliff. It was just another cliff in another bleak landscape. It was probably enchanting seeing it all under the light of the midnight sun, but I'd be damned if I was going to stay here another night if I could help it.

I was sore and homesick. It's a shame really, and now, provided with the space of close to forty years, and viewed through the lens of the safety of home, I fervently wished that I had taken more time to really live and enjoy the moment. When I visited, I remember that the reason to be there was for the challenge, the experience, to be able to shout out the claim that, at least for a moment or two, you were the northernmost and probably the moistest motorcyclist in the entirety of Europe.

Nowadays the visitor centre charges 130 Krona to enter. That's $30 USD or £25 GBP per person. If the view is obscured by cloud or fog (hint: it often is) you don't get a refund, but you can revisit for free within 24 hours. There has even been a recent court case, brought by the government, about charging visitors, so the owners made the worst concession, possibly in history. If you arrive by bicycle or on foot you get in free. Bicycle or walk—I ask you? I had the use of a 1000cc motorcycle and travelled in the middle of summer. I barely made it. How are you supposed to walk there? They don't even allow foot traffic through the tunnel that now serves the island, and the ferry service has long since been discontinued.

Back at the container I found the Germans all packing up their belongings onto bikes that had been pulled up outside. They had seen the weather and had agreed with me, to get off the island and head south before the next storm rolled through and locked us all down again.

I re-packed my bike and stuck my little sticker onto the side of my helmet. My sticky memento bore an image of the iron globe and the simultaneously iconic and ironic words 'Land of the Midnight Sun' worded around the circumference. I spread my map on the floor of the container and thought about where to go next. My original plan had been to initially ride south for a hundred miles and then ride east through Finland until I reached the border with Russia. I couldn't actually enter Russia; I didn't have the correct visas to do so.

Communism was in its final death throes, but it was still a lingering and potent menace that kept borders closed. But still, I thought it would be cool to peer through the barbed wire at the border, to be able to at least say I had 'seen' Russia. As I pondered the extra time and mileage it would take, Georgie came up and asked me what I was planning, and I told him. He looked at me like I had gone insane.

"Wait. So, you are just going to ride all that way, hundreds of miles to the border of Russia, but not actually go inside?"

"Yes. That's the plan."

There was a long silence.

"But why?"

He had a good point and I thought he made it well. Why on earth would I do such a thing to myself. For the same reason I had ridden all this way to look at a cliff for thirty seconds or so I suppose. But he was right. We were both bruised and battered, our precious bikes had been damaged, and we both still had a couple of thousand miles left to ride. It was time to start the long road home. Georgie asked me to ride with him and Ella, at least for a little while, and thankful for his offer and the promise of good company I readily agreed.

Mosquitos

Resembling a rag-tag post-apocalyptic motorcycle gang from Mad Max, Georgie, Ella, the rest of the Germans and myself, all rode away from Nordkapp together. If there had been any towns to ride through, children would have been pulled inside from playing in the streets, windows barred, and doors locked. But as it was, our passing went unnoticed by all but the Arctic Hares.

We re-traced our steps along the winding road that had been hidden in yesterday's storm. Every now and again the sea would appear as a flash between the headlands, a shining distant disk. Georgie wanted to stop where we had been blown off the road. He still thought that his sleeping bags might be found. Who knows where he thought they might be in this barren wilderness. Stuck on the velvet covered antlers of a passing reindeer perhaps. I told him they were almost certain to be wrapped around a TV antenna in Murmansk by now, but he was adamant.

As a group we all patiently granted him his personal odyssey. We stopped a few times while Georgie paced up and down the road looking for signs of where we had left the road and any meaningful detritus that might lead him to the discovery of his precious sleeping bags. But in the end, we couldn't even find the location of the accident. We disagreed on how close to the ferry port the crash had occurred, I was adamant that it was closer, and Georgie was equally certain it had been nearer Nordkapp. In the excitement and adrenalin overload of the accident, our memories had been compromised. In the end, there was no evidence of the incident we could see, even in the clear light of the day and Georgie finally went quiet and gave up the search.

We all parked up at the ferry terminal to wait for the ferry to return. We stood and sat in the sunshine. The day was still, and the weak sun leant its unexpected, but welcome, warmth to our chilled bodies. Leather jackets were removed, and waterproofs stashed. We all steamed in the sunshine like racehorses, basking in the drying heat.

Cigarettes were lit and shared, and we all sat around in the inexplicable sunshine like a bunch of English biker friends who had ridden twenty fast miles to a café at the top of the Cat and Fiddle to enjoy a bacon sandwich, not some mismatched and very weird looking bunch of European strangers waiting for a ferry at the very ends of the earth.

We had to wait about twenty-minutes before the ferry pulled up, and after it had docked and lowered its ramp, we watched the cars and four or five motorcyclists ride down the clanking ramp. The bikers all looked dry and happy and gave us all a cheery wave as they headed off to complete the last few miles of their journey to Nordkapp. Their timing had been so much better than ours, and while we all waved back, it was difficult to hide our open hatred through teeth pulled back in disdain.

The ferry journey was pleasant enough. We all crowded the rail at the back of the ship to look back with sad eyes as the island of Magerøya sank over the horizon.

Yesterday, during the storm, the cliffs had seemed menacing. Dangerous and brooding they lurked like the promise of a premonition. A threat. This morning, they seemed pleasant and verdant underneath a blue sky slashed with cirrostratus. We could have been on the south coast of England on an early spring day. The sea was mockingly flat and placid, the small ripples shone back the unexpected brilliance of the day in a twinkling dance that blinded our eyes. It had been our fate to win through in that hard battle to our destination, but it had not been our time to enjoy it.

In the morning sun the journey was short and easy, and soon enough, with a roar of engines and a blast of her horn the ferry maneuvered to gently dock. We rode the bikes off the ferry and then parked in a rough semi-circle in the middle of the ferry terminal. Our bad parking annoyed the disembarking cars that had to swerve around us. Being British, being badly parked annoyed me as well and I really wanted, deep down to move my bike into one of the clearly marked, and available, parking bays. But I felt at this point that I was now part of this rough, tough biker gang. I just had to suck it up and show my rebellious side.

We got off the bikes and Georgie, Ella and myself exchanged handshakes and hugs as we all said our goodbyes to the rest of the Germans. I would ride with Georgie and Ella through Finland and then Sweden, but the rest of the Germans had come to Nordkapp along that route. Their long and twisting path home lay along the western road, through the twisting, strangulated knot of fjords of Norway that we had already passed through.

All of our paths lay together for a little while longer, but this would be our last chance to speak our farewells and pass on wishes of better luck for the rest of each other's journeys.

For the first part of the morning, we all rode together alongside the shore of the vast Porsangerfjorden we had ridden in on. I had the much bigger and faster bike and got promoted to take point navigating the way. Georgie and Ella were behind me, and the rest of our rag tag bunch strung out behind me like a string of two-wheeled multi-coloured prayer flags.

As I rode, I paid close attention to the mirrors. At first, I rode slowly. I was a mother duck making sure her brood was always safe and close behind her. But as the group continued to stay together, I pushed the pace, faster and faster. Soon we were flying.

With the sun out and only the slightest of breezes and absolutely no other traffic, the ride was an enjoyable sweep of fast bends and swooping switchbacks, long climbs and hair-raising descents into valleys filled with streams that tumbled frost coated granite boulders down to the ever-present fjord.

Considering the variety of bikes and riders, we would have made a pretty good display team, so in-synch we were as we swooped through the valleys and mountain passes. It was as if our shared misfortune and the combination of the joyous semi-drunken night in the container had created a single entity of speed and ability.

Close to Olderfjord we turned inland to follow the course of the fast-flowing River Goahtemuorjohka. For mile after mile, we crossed and re-crossed the river. At times it was a furious, primordial surge of wild white water, at others a broad and placid ribbon of melt water from the distant mountains.

At the town of Kronstad the road finally split us. We all came to stop, as a group, in the middle of the empty road at an unnecessarily broad T-junction. The road the Germans had chosen lay to the west, and ours to the southeast, towards Finland. Visors were lifted, and smiles were shared and then, in a cacophony of tooted horns and raised hands we signalled our final farewells. The day was brought alive with the sudden roar of engines as the feral Germans peeled away, one at a time, to turn right at the junction and then sudden silence fell, as they disappeared one at a time around the sweeping bend.

I nodded to Georgie, and we pulled away together, southeast towards the distant border with Finland.

It would be a long ride; we had many miles to cover. But the weather remained good, and the roads were well paved, smooth, and fast. As we moved deeper into the country, farther from the coast, all of the lovely crinkly edges faded away, replaced by a flat country filled with small coldly reflective lakes.

We had entered the truly vast area called Finnmarksvidda, Norway's largest highland plateau, an enormous area of more than eight-thousand-five-hundred square miles. There were over ten-thousand lakes in the region. Some smaller but many large and impressive. They all sparkled in the rare sunshine of the afternoon. As we rode deeper and deeper into the region, the fresh and chilly air of the plateau whistled down the collar of my leather jacket. I reached up a gloved hand to try and pull the zipper tighter and as I did so the splatter of a heavy bodied bug landed with a loud 'whump' on my visor.

For those smart enough not to have ridden motorcycles, particularly in colder countries, you may be happily ignorant of some of the pleasures you have spared yourself. Things like hands so cold and wet that when you remove sodden gloves, each of your fingers resemble Lord Voldemort's shrivelled foreskin. Or a back so pained and cramping, and so squeezed into a torturously tight set of leathers that, after you get off the bike at the end of the day, you walk for the first thirty minutes like Quasimodo with legs so bandy you couldn't stop an ungreased pig in an alley, all viewed through a visor permanently fogged, iced, drenched, scratched, or in this case, smudged with the dead bodies and streaked blood of insects.

One bug became two and then two became ten and within seconds we were entirely enveloped by a dark swarm of large, fat-bodied mosquitos. I swear they were the size and heft of starlings. I was suddenly riding through a seething, roiling, madly whining murmuration of blood sucking fiends.

I attempted to wipe the dead bodies away with a gloved hand but only managed to smear the tiny legs and blood further across my vision. It soon became much worse. We were riding headlong into an area in which people, including the hardy Suni, and even reindeer and other animals, simply choose to abandon during the summer months to escape the hordes of ravenous mosquitos that spring into life there.

The myriad, endless lakes and relatively warm weather are perfect breeding grounds to jiggle the infant larvae into writhing pupa and then into virulent and bitey adult life. I read somewhere that there are 110 *trillion* mosquitos in the world. That is 16,000 mosquitos for every human alive on the planet. Well, for some reason, I can assure you, that on that day at least a trillion of the bastard things, had converged on that one single spot for an all you can eat damp biker buffet.

We were soon riding through a dense dark cloud of them. They filled the air around us, a ravenous, high-pitched whining fog. I could see Georgie behind me desperately wiping his visor, and swatting the creatures, alternating hands as he did so. Behind him I could see Ella doing the same thing. From my perspective it comically looked like Vishnu was riding the bike behind me.

The mass of mosquitos was so dense that despite the few yards that separated us Georgie was disappearing, being consumed within the cloud of tiny flying bodies.

Outside the small town of Masi, we had to pull over for gas. A cloud of the mosquitos hovered around my helmeted head. I must have looked like Pig Pen or Dirty McSquirty. I put the bike into neutral to unfasten and remove my helmet. The air was alive with a loud high-pitched buzzing whine that completely enveloped us. It was deafening. The sound was rhythmic, it rose and fell in pitch and intensity. We were soon covered in black biting bodies, the bikes, our leathers and then, our hands and faces. I couldn't believe the feral Germans wouldn't have offered a single warning about this. They must have passed along this very road and surely had been subjected to the same misery.

We were rendered into a thrashing, madly waving spectacle as we tried to hastily pump petrol into the bikes. The bites stung at first and then itched furiously.

"Why didn't the other Germans warn us about this?" I shouted across to Georgie as we writhed and flailed at the cloud that hovered and swarmed around us as we watched the needles on the pump slowly tick Krone by expensive Krone to fill the tanks.

Georgie didn't answer and when I turned to face him, he looked awkwardly and comically sheepish.

I raised an eyebrow. "They did, didn't they?"

"Ja. Sorry. I forgot to mention it. They said whatever you do, don't even think about coming this way. Go any other way, ride through Russia if you have to, just don't come this way. I thought they were exaggerating," he finished meekly with a shrug of his broad shoulders and an embarrassed grin on his big and increasingly red-welted face.

"For fucks sake Georgie," I shouted. The bike was finally full, and I dashed into the store to hand over a truly eye watering and exorbitant amount of cash to the attendant. Back outside I quickly pulled my helmet and gloves back on and tore off in a childishly hissy fit of dust and small stones.

The rest of the day we rode through the haze of fat busy circling bodies. The bikes and our leathers continued to collect tiny corpses, little spots of black and red. It wasn't long before every square inch of us and the bits of the bikes that faced forwards were plastered in them. Our visors continued to become welted and smeared until we were left peering out of tiny gaps between the bodies, squint eyed through the gloom they left behind, like impatient drivers on a hard frost morning.

We finally found a campsite just outside the town of Kautokeino. Personally, I could go no further. My ribs hurt and my shoulder throbbed. My eyes burned from squinting for mile after interminable mile through the blood smeared detritus of a hundred-thousand dead mosquitos. Wherever the mosquitos had made ingress, and even through the leathers, there were many, I had a spectacular and maddening array of itches that could not be scratched while I was riding.

We parked the bikes and then, like astronauts on a spacewalk we awkwardly unpacked and erected our tents in full leathers, gloves and helmets. The mosquitos were drawn to us as we sweated and easily found every piece of unprotected, pink virgin skin. Our necks and the backs of our heads were soon covered in their ravenous blood-engorged, eagerly feasting bodies. They found egress under the smallest of gaps at the ankles and wrists of our leathers creating red and itching bracelets there.

I was still really pissed off with Georgie.

I stopped for a moment and thought about that for a long second. Actually, I wasn't angry with Georgie at all. I was angry with myself. Myself, and the whole situation that had confronted us across the last few days. Georgie was just a very large, easy and readily available target for my wrath.

I was really angry about the crash, the cold, the damage to my bike and myself. The unexpected appearance of the several billion vampiric bugs that seemed intent on draining us of blood hadn't helped, I had to admit. But the reality was, that even if I had known about the mosquito riddled highlands we were traversing, I would still have chosen this path. It was the route that I wanted to take, and in those days, logic and common sense seldom stood in my way. If I had known that a furious, club-wielding Troll lay in wait for me on this road I would still have come.

But it did begin to feel that all of my choices were leading us out of one frying pan and into an increasingly hotter one.

But admitting to myself that I was the asshole, didn't mean that I was ready to admit that to Georgie. Not yet. We put up our tents with the openings facing each other, a grudging thirty feet or so apart, in silent recognition of our tiff. Once inside I zipped up the door and stripped out of my leathers, slapping, brushing, panting and sweating until I was certain that every insect, I had inadvertently brought in with me, was positively dead.

I put on some music on my Walkman, '*The Bangles — Eternal Flame*,' and checked my panniers to see if I had any supplies left. Not much. A couple of packets of dehydrated soup, a stale bun and three hard boiled eggs. Eternal Flame ended and '*Nena—99 Red Balloons*' started up. After a few seconds, from the tent opposite I heard Ella start to softly sing along to the music, but in her native tongue, the original German it had been written in. She had a good voice.

"*Neunundneunzig Luftballons*
Auf ihrem Weg zum Horizont
Hielt man fuer UFOs aus dem All
Darum schickte ein General
Eine Fliegerstaffel hinterher
Alarm zu geben, wenn es so war
Dabei war da am Horizont
Nur Neunundneunzig Luftballons"

I suddenly felt bad at swearing at Georgie like this was all his fault. I pictured his enormous square head with the sad, puppy dog eyes looking back at me like I had kicked him for pissing on the rug. I sat stewing in reluctance to admit my bad behaviour for a while but then admitted defeat.

Keeping the tent door tightly zipped, I blindly shouted across the short space.

"Hey Georgie!"

"Ja Andy, wie geht's? What's up?"

"You have any food?"

"Etwas. A little, yes. Some cheese, some chocolate."

"Cool. I can make some soup and I have some eggs if you would like to share?"

"I think that would be nice." There was a guilty pause. "Hey man, I am sorry…"

"No mate. I'm sorry. Sorry for being a verdammt wichsen. That's the right phrase yeah?"

"Ja. You learn German really quickly. Come over to our tent and we will eat together. We will have us a Viking feast."

To get across to Georgie and Ella's tent I had to put on my personal spacesuit of jeans, leather jacket, gloves, and helmet to sprint the few feet across the opening. Georgie was ready with the tent flaps, held partly open like and air lock to admit me entry and then, with me safely inside, he immediately sealed the opening against unwanted insectile intrusion.

That night we sat inside the tent together, chatting and listening to my poor choices in music and eating our slightly odd do-it-yourself meal. Outside, the sun hung in the sky, brushing the tree line. It would have been pleasant to have been able to sit outside and enjoy the midnight sun, but the constant, deafening whine of the menacing blood-thirsty horde that never relented in its unceasing attack on the thin protection of the fabric of the tent was sufficient to keep us terrified and firmly inside.

FINLAND

The morning brought a light drizzle. For once on this endless, rain swept journey, I was happy to hear the patter of droplets on the tent. The cool of the rain had brought a dash of welcome relief from the mosquitos. We packed up while the coffee brewed, carefully cleaned visors, and chiselled congealed bits of dead bugs from headlights and fairings.

Georgie led us away from the campsite. We stopped for gas and supplies at a Circle K just south of the town of Kautokeino and then got back on the road. The mosquito bites from the previous day itched furiously, particularly the ones at my ankles and wrists where the leathers rubbed. It was infuriating as nothing could be scratched, it was a constant and maddening distraction all morning as we rode south.

The terrain remained much the same as the previous day. Flat with small, stunted trees, wind twisted gorse with small yellow flowers and thorn covered bushes that lined the road. Lakes lay all around us, glimmering in the sunshine that had finally replaced the morning showers. The scenery really didn't change all morning, the road was straight, and towns and houses were a rare sight.

It was mid-morning when we crossed into Finland. There was no hard border, no barriers or customs officer to hand a passport to, just a sign with a single word 'Suomi' the Finnish word for Finland, printed white on blue and surrounded by gold stars.

It was wilderness in every direction. In fact, much of this part of Finland is officially designated and protected as wilderness. There are twelve such areas in Finland today covering 5,750 square miles and the road we were on was surrounded on both sides by two of them, the Tarvanto-varran and the Pöyrisjärvi Wilderness Areas.

In a world where true wilderness is becoming a rarity and land exploitation more and more common, I thought it splendid that Finland had the foresight to invest in a project that seeks to simply preserve the very character and definition of wilderness itself. Wilderness in Finland, in that time and place, encompassed not only the pretty, remote lakes, and the barren, seemingly endless expanse of Reindeer munched tundra, it also extended to include and protect both the Sámi culture and the Sámi's natural form of livelihood. I thought that was very thoughtful, beautiful, and tender. Very Scandinavian.

The entire vista was ruggedly and emptily beautiful. But man, after the first fourteen hours or so of marvelling at the whole emptiness of rugged nature, it is a whole lot of nothing to ride through all day.

We reached the border with Sweden in the early after-noon but quickly realized we now faced a dilemma. The natural border between Finland and Sweden is formed by the mighty River Tonio which runs broadly south and east for three-hundred and forty-five miles along the fron-tier. The road we were travelling on suddenly ended at a T-junction as it met the river. In front of us across the wide expanse of river lay Sweden. It lay on the other side. We could see Sweden, tantalizingly close, through the thin strand of trees on the far bank. But there was no bridge across the river to allow us direct entry to the country.

We were forced to choose between either turning right, which would take us north to ride thirty miles out of our way to the bridge crossing at the town of Karesuvanto and then cut through the very middle of Sweden or turn left to follow the river south for two-hundred and sixty miles to cross into Sweden at the bridge at Tornio, where the river the town is named for gives issue into the Gulf of Bothnia. From there we would ride the pretty road that runs along the gulf, south, all the way to Stockholm. Neither Georgie nor I had decided, or even discussed, which was the preferred route.

The T-junction was clearly one of those locations where many such decisions of import had been made, as out of all of the wilderness and emptiness we had ridden through, it suddenly sported both a petrol station and, conveniently, a small café.

We parked the bikes and crunched our way across the gravel of the car park. The café was dark inside. Timber built with a long bar at one end and an array of cheap wooden furniture scattered about. Lanterns hung from low rafters, each lit with a candle that guttered with a yellow flame. It was mostly empty, just one other table was occupied by three long-distance truckers, so we three sat at a large table and spread my map wide across the worn wood of the tabletop. The young woman who served us was Sámi, dressed in the traditional colourful Gakti. She took our order and quickly returned with our coffees in three large and steaming mugs.

There were merits to both paths, but on checking distances, I favoured the more direct route through central Sweden. I was on a time budget and still wanted to ride back through Denmark and spend some time with a friend in Holland on the way home. Georgie and Ella had set their hearts on spending a few days in Stockholm and from there they had a more direct route to Gothenburg where they could get a ferry back to Kiel in Germany. We chatted about it for quite a while.

It was a difficult decision and for quite a while we danced around the obvious choices that needed to be made, but we decided that, in the end, we would have to part ways. It was strange. I had only known them for a few days, although it was fair to say they had been days both eventful and rendered forever memorable for a variety of reasons.

We sipped our coffees slowly, eking out the last moments of our time together. When the empty coffee mugs were finally banged down on the top of the wooden trestle table it marked the time to part. We were suddenly reluctant to say our goodbyes. We exchanged actual postal addresses, because emails were beginning to become popular, but were not quite ubiquitous yet. Back in the car park, where the rain had begun, once more, to fall in big fat drops, I hugged both Georgie and Ella hard and told them to ride safely. I watched them mount their much too small bike, and while I pulled on my gloves and helmet, they turned out of the parking lot and with a last wave they headed south. I watched Ella's orange waterproof disappear into the far distance until it was consumed by the trees and turned with a forlorn sigh.

I felt immediately alone in this vast and empty country. I was still at least a four-day ride from Holland, mostly on roads where I would seldom see another soul, and my spirits were perhaps as low on that trip as they had ever been. I admit I felt very lost and sorry for myself.

With another long sigh I got back on my Kawasaki. Not for the first time on a long biking trip I wished I had a rental car. I could have just driven back to the nearest airport, bought a ticket and took a fast flight home. By nightfall I could have been safely back in my Mum's house running a hot bath while she fussed around me making me my favourite tea, a full-English fry up or one of her amazing homemade meat pies.

But every long journey, both outwards towards the thrill of the unknown and the gut-wrenching draw of the adventure, or even back towards the comfort of home starts with that first, sometimes reluctant mile. So, I pulled in the clutch, fired up the bike and cogged it into first gear. I slipped the clutch as I rolled out of the car park and, instead of following Georgie and Ella south, I turned back towards the north.

That first mile was the hardest. Riding away from friends and towards loneliness, and who knew what the new road might bring. But the miles slowly slipped by, as they always do, and the tether that bound us together slowly loosened, a tight rubber band at first, but incrementally, mile after mile, becoming a thinner and thinner elastic strand. A connection that once made will never break but will always tie two travellers together. A bond formed of shared experience.

I rolled the throttle back and let the Kawasaki do its job as I cogged up through the gearbox, the exhaust a lupine howl in the wilderness. I really needed to get some mileage under my belt if I was going to be able to see all that I still wanted to see.

I followed the river towards the small town of Karesuvanto and then, without any sign of a border guard, I was swept across the bridge that spans the Tornio River and into Sweden. Another T-junction took me left to return me back onto my southward path.

The highland plateau shifted so gradually from barren, lake dotted wilderness to a green tunnel of conifers that the transition seemed sudden to me even though it must have occurred over the span of one hundred miles or more.

That night I camped at a small site north of Jokkmokk. The site would be my last night inside the Arctic Circle.

Set amidst towering pines I set up the tent and put a Billycan of water to boil on my little stove to make some soup. I was all alone on the site and as evening fell there wasn't a sound to be heard, save the unremitting patter of rain on my tent and the relentless, drip, drip of rain slipping from the heavy tree limbs that hung, saturated, bowed to the ground. Even the high wind in the tops of the firs had hushed and the birds had lost their song.

I sat in the opening of my tent sipping my vegetable soup and peeling a boiled egg when I heard a heavy snort and a cracking of twigs. Northern Sweden is home to Brown bears, wolves, lynx and wolverines and my blood ran cold as I sat stock still, my lip scorching cup of soup held up to my mouth, moving my head slowly, from side to side, trying to fix precisely where the sound had come from. Another crash and then a loud crack almost directly behind me.

I tried to decide if it was safer to get back in the tent, close my eyes and just wait for the end to come, or to flee in a vain attempt to summon help from the empty road, when the creature decided for me. It stepped out of the tree line with a disdainful casualness, and then stood still, barely ten feet from me. A male reindeer. But this one was unlike the ones I had seen with their Sámi herders. This spectacular specimen was close to five feet tall at the shoulders and must have weighed five hundred pounds. His rack of antlers was as long as he was tall, his myriad points were wide and spatula shaped, heavily coated in velvet they arced gracefully, a perfect weapon for protection. His pelt was thick and shaggy. It hung in curls and tangles around his broad neck and shoulders. His coat was snow white beneath his throat but darkly mottled and tousled across his back and deeply muscled hind quarters. He smelled of the tundra and of the wilderness, of musk and peat and hoary frost and broken bracken.

He seemed to notice me for the first time, or perhaps he was simply aware of who this part of the forest truly belonged to and how poorly equipped with antler defences I surely was. He looked at me out of the corner of one dark and glassy eye for several seconds. I could see my own reflection, a small damp-looking figure looking back at me, seated perfectly still. He puffed out a loud snort of air that fogged instantly in the cold of the evening. His breath hung in the air for a long moment and then it slipped away on the gentle breeze. With that, he looked away from me and walked casually across the short meadow to slip serenely back into the woods.

I realized that I had neither moved the cup of hot soup from my mouth, or taken a breath during the entire encounter, and now I took in a huge, ragged gulp of air to fill my lungs and cool burnt lips.

So Many Pines

In the morning, after packing and making coffee in the rain I set off once more. I stopped in the town of Jokkmokk to refuel. As well as being a small wooden dining table and chair set available to buy from Ikea, Jokkmokk is also an important cultural centre for the Sámi people. It is home to around three-thousand people and carries the name given to it by the Lule Sámi tribe, composed as it is of the individual words jåhkå and måhkke, meaning *'River's Curve.'* There has been a large market there every Thursday since the year 1605, with a fair, concerts and exhibitions and I would love to describe it more fully, but of course I passed through on a Friday.

I rode south for barely thirty minutes and then by the side of the road I stopped for a little while to take a photo of the road sign that marked my entry back inside, to the warmer and more civilized side, of the Arctic Circle. If anything, in Sweden it was marked with even less fanfare. I was the only one on the road that even stopped to take note. It felt good to be back in more temperate climbs, the weather was still chilly, and the rain had intensified all morning as I had ridden, but every mile would now carry me further and further southward, closer to home, larger towns, and the chance of better weather. It felt like reaching a summit. The only way now was down.

I passed through the small village of Tårrajaur that stood on the edge of a lake that glittered like a knife edge in the rare ray of sunshine that managed to temporarily struggle free of the blanket of cloud. Ten miles further down the road I was swallowed by a vast forest. I thought that after a few tens of miles I would break free again and once more see rugged hills and sparkling lakes. The entire terrain of Norway had kept me engaged and interested. From the moment I rode down from the ferry in Bergen to my crossing into Finland, I had been constantly engrossed in its endlessly changing landscapes. Norway had shifted between pretty fjords, breath-taking ascents and descents, high windswept and barren plains, low fertile valleys, and lofty, snow-capped mountains.

But little did I know, central Sweden is literally just filled with trees. I rode all day through that green tunnel of damp and dripping conifers. It was like riding through the largest Christmas Tree display on the planet.

There were few signs of civilization, almost no cars, few towns, just a single endless wet ribbon of tarmac that stretched out to infinity in front of me. Even the roads were mostly straight and without variation. Pines grew tall all around me, hemmed me in, restricted my view to only the road in front of me and the forest at my side. Even when the road rose high enough to give me sight of the countryside below me, it was a huge seamless, carpet of pines. A forest of the elder days, when the world was blanketed, horizon to horizon in every direction with trees. A time and a place where man had yet to come with his flinted axes and his kindling fire.

Bob Ross would have loved it there, so many happy little trees, and they had all brought ten thousand friends, but it was a tedious landscape to ride through, it was relentlessly repetitive and claustrophobic. At times I felt that, perhaps I had gotten myself lost in this arboreal terrain. Turned endlessly around, tricked by the timeless trees into constantly turning back into the snaring depths of the forest's branches and roots. It felt Tolkein like to me, Frodo and Sam led astray to be lost forever in distant Mirkwood.

Part of me expected to see Tom Bombadil chatting with Treebeard, back in a lost age before the time of men, both young again, in an age when the Old Forest was not quite so ancient.

And if you didn't get that reference, shame on you.

I rode in that manner, mindlessly, no distraction to be seen. I was lost within my own thoughts, which is seldom a good place to be for too long. I was surrounded on every side by greenery. Like being trapped forever inside a badly maintained fish tank, I rode through the rain blanketed forest during the day and camped, ate boiled eggs, and slept in the forest at night.

The rain during the day was maddening. Upon entering the forest of Sweden, as I was beginning to think of it, the clouds had gathered, hiding the sun in a heavy gruel of thick, swirling grey clouds that at times touched the treetops themselves. It dripped, drizzled, trinkled and sprinkled. A constant wetness that permeated the air itself. It clattered down on me from the trees above; it splashed up from the road as I swept wetly by. It was a constant drenching companion.

If the rain during the day was maddening, the rain at night, as it dropped heavily from the high branches and onto the thin polyester of my tent was beginning to drive me insane. It was a Chinese water torture tuned to a hair pulling infrequency. Discordant and sporadic, the rain pooled on the topmost leaves and the pinecones above me and then fell, one hundred feet of momentum to land on the tent like a toddler hitting a runcible spoon on a large tin pan, again and again and again.

It became impossible to sleep well. Wherever I accidently touched the surface of the tent, a drip would begin to fall from that spot, slowly soaking the groundsheet and everything it touched. Which was mostly me, but also my sleeping bag. The clothes I managed to keep mainly dry inside the panniers, but what with the insufferable rain during the day's ride and the leaky tent at night, I was once more, wetter than a cucumber in a women's prison.

Everything around me, every hour, every minute and every second of every day was relentlessly green. Like an old valve TV that had lost its blue and red contrast my world was a verdant monotone. Ferns, bushes, trees and brush. Green, green, green, green, green. Sweden had captured the monopoly on the colour. It literally had all of the shades. Lincoln, olive, pea, sage, emerald, lime and bottle, and quite a few others my thesaurus simply gave up on.

Of course I had even brought a green tent, so even when I climbed into my sleeping bag at night the 'roof,' so to speak was also bloody green.

As I say, I think I was beginning to lose the plot, my cheese about to fall off my cracker as the saying goes. My only motivation to get back on the bike and to keep riding each morning became to eventually escape this endlessly emerald arboreal prison.

As I rode south the mix of trees gradually shifted from exclusively pine to predominantly pine, some spruce and the occasional birch. It was no relief whatsoever. I fervently wished that I had followed Georgie and Ella and taken the coast road south to Stockholm. I was so dejected and bored I even opened up my map and calculated roughly where they might be. I figured that if they had made similar progress to me, they would be close to the Högakusten-bron bridge a little north of the town of Sundsvall. The terrain there would be pretty I was certain. Lakes and little inlets to cross, with far flung views of the Gulf of Bothnia dotted with clusters of small islands, and pastel coloured shipping smacks, all set under clear blue skies.

But I also knew I had once more taken the least favoured path with good reason. I soon had to be back at work. How wonderful it must be to have no limits on budget, time, and responsibilities, to just point the front wheel at some distant vista and keep on going. But, for me, there was no alternative, I was committed to this leafy path.

It wasn't until close to the end of day three when the forest faltered for the first time. I glimpsed a field through the thinning trees. The open space disappeared as the trees closed back up around me and then, suddenly, a vast corn field unfolded in front of me. I blinked the verdancy from my eyes and drank in the colours, the gold of the swaying corn, the red roofed barn, the gleaming white walls of the town that peeped over the top of the gently sloping hill in the far distance. I actually pulled the bike over to stare, breathlessly and with great relief to have escaped the endless greenery. I took a moment to let my eyes and other senses flow out to welcome the space and openness, to blink away the monotony of the endless forest.

I filled up the bike with petrol at a town called Grums, bought some supplies and found a little campsite close to Skoghall on the shore of the gargantuan Lake Vänern, the largest lake in the European Union. Lake Vänern covers an area of over 2,183 square miles and has given life and prosperity to the cluster of small towns that have thrived around it based on the tourism and fishing industries the lake provides. I was just happy to be out of the fucking woods.

I celebrated by drinking a couple of ten quid beers and adding two slices of wafer-thin ham to my nightly boiled egg. After dinner I didn't feel too well. The expensive and extremely lively lager had interacted in some foulsome manner with the eggs. I was bloated and had severe stomach cramps. I went for a walk along the shore of the lake to see if I could walk off the upset.

It was very pretty and serene. I saw a blue tourist sign for something labelled '*Hammarö Sydspets – 2km,*' and not having any idea what that might be, decided to walk the two kilometres to find out. The path meandered into a heavily wooded area which, after the last three days of riding through endless forests, initially crushed my spirits, but I decided I would press on regardless.

I climbed a steep shale path, and the trees were suddenly swept aside like dramatic velvet stage curtains to reveal the white brick built Skage lighthouse at the very southern promontory of Hammarö. The vastness of Lake Vänern stretched out beneath me, a darkly reflective shimmer of blue marble. A white-tailed eagle flew low across the water, its wing tips touched and sent little concentric rings to ripple gently across the surface. A little dopple of Goosanders lay far out, their mirror images paddling furiously along beneath them.

I was happy even though my stomach still hurt. The sun was beginning to set. I had travelled one-thousand miles since I had crossed the Arctic Circle and the more southerly latitude meant that night would soon fall. I started my walk back to the campsite and dusk soon fell around me to darken the rough ground at my feet. My stomach growled and then gave a disturbingly loud and liquid sounding gurgle, like a blocked drain being internally unblocked.

I began to hurry through the woods, back to my campsite, as I was certain that I would soon be needing its facilities. Halfway back to camp a cramp doubled me over. I looked around. The wood was deserted. Certain I was alone, I lifted a leg to, very carefully, set free what I fervently hoped would be just some trapped wind. The sound was impressive. It began with a high-pitched whistle but ended with a robust and fern rattling bugle sound. The animal sounds of the forest were immediately silenced, sure that, somewhere a Goosander was in certain distress.

The relief was immediate. Unfortunately, a young Swedish couple had been canoodling in the darkness of the undergrowth beside me and they both looked up in horror, hands clamped over mouths at the sound and subsequent miasma.

I muttered a quiet and very English "sorry," and with cheeks blushing at both ends I hurried back to my solitary campsite.

A Flirtation

I was still feeling a little ropey in the morning, but I had another hard-boiled egg for breakfast and while I boiled some water from the lake to make coffee, I pulled out my map and spread it across the floor of my cramped and increasingly damp and malodorous tent. It was raining again. The low clouds captured the tops of the conifers in its grey embrace; yet another miserable day of riding in the rain awaited me.

While the rain drummed an endless staccato beat on the tent above me, I looked at my travel options. My original plan, such as it was, was to ride almost to the southern tip of Sweden, to the town of Malmo and to catch the car ferry across to Copenhagen and enter Denmark there. If, as exists today, there had been the splendid Øresund Bridge that now whisks traffic between Denmark and Sweden across the Øresund strait I probably would have continued with that plan. But given I had to catch a ferry anyway, I now thought that catching the Gothenburg ferry to Frederikshavn in the north of Denmark, the one the Danish tourers I had met on my way north had taken, might be a better and simpler choice.

I think a big part of me just wanted to leave Sweden behind. I am certain that was grossly unfair of me. Sweden surely has many fine things to recommend it, ABBA, IKEA, meatballs and the chef from the Muppets immediately spring to mind, but the interminable ride through the pine forests had adversely coloured my opinion. I wanted a change of scenery and at the least, a short respite from this long, lonely and tiring ride. I figured that if I took the Gothenburg ferry, I could find, and possibly even afford an actual hotel in Denmark. One with a bed and a roof and even, perhaps, a bath with hot water. I could hang up my helmet and riding gloves for a day or so and recuperate, at least give my troubled digestive system a break from eggs and life on the road.

With that decision made I felt enormously better, like a huge weight had been lifted from my shoulders. Another strange thing had happened, for the first time in almost five days, the sound of the rain's relentless patter had ceased.

I poked my head out of the flap and looked up into an almost clear blue sky.

Perhaps I had angered Freyr, the Norse god of weather in my initial ride north of Bergen. Perhaps I should have sacrificed a boar as the Vikings would have done to secure safe passage. Regardless, with my decision to leave Sweden finally made, the Gods were finally appeased. I gave a nod to the sky above, thankful that at last she approved of my new plan. I packed up the tent and re-packed the bike.

It was only two-hundred or so miles to Gothenburg and most of the road ran alongside, or in close proximity to Lake Vänern. Beech trees hid the lake for most of the ride, but I was happy to be out, sun glinting off the bike, wind buffeting my helmet, warm hands and feet and a full tank of fuel between my legs. It was a fine day to be out riding.

I made Gothenburg by lunchtime. The city sparkled in the midday sun. The layout of Gothenburg resembles many Dutch cities. The roads and canals are laid out in a similar design to that of Amsterdam and even, would you believe it, Jakarta in Indonesia. The reason is that Dutch engineers built all three cities. Gothenburg was originally a Dutch trading colony which somewhat strangely also attracted many Scots to locate there early in its history. William Chalmers, the son of a Scottish immigrant, donated his fortunes to set up what later became the Chalmers University of Technology and in 1841, the Scotsman Alexander Keiller founded the Götaverken shipbuilding company that was in business there until 1989.

The city only fully acceded to Sweden in 1621 when the last Dutch politician on the city board passed away. Today it is a huge industrial city, home to Volvo and a handsome university.

The port was busy and as I parked the bike and walked to find the ticket office to enquire about times and prices for the ferry across to Frederikshavn, I found myself subconsciously looking for Georgie and Ella's little bike parked amongst the scramble of cars. I knew it was highly unlikely that they would be here at the same time, they were surely still having fun in Stockholm, but I couldn't stop myself hoping to find them there.

The ticket office handed me my ticket and pointed to a large Stena Line ferry just navigating her approach through the broad channel of the Göta älv river. I jogged back to the bike just as the other passengers began to start their engines and I took my place in line. There must be some mutual affinity between ferry operators and motorcyclists, as I felt a tap on my shoulder and one of the uniformed stewards motioned me to move forward to the front of the line, so as usual I was first to board.

One of the crew helped me secure the bike to an anchor point in the bowels of the car deck and I took my tank bag, containing cash and passport, with me up the steep steel stairs. I left my panniers on the bike. I figured that if some desperate Scandinavian thief could find profit from the socks and underpants that festered within, then hey, good luck to him.

I walked upwards and forwards to find a seat at the prow of the ship on an upper deck so that I could relax and enjoy the view and the two and a half-hour journey across the Kategatt, the stretch of fairly shallow seawater that separates Sweden from Denmark. The sea there is so shallow and filled with sandy and stony reefs, that continuously shift in the tricky current, that artificial trenches have been dug to safeguard the large amount of international traffic that traverses it each day.

The ferry was soon filled with passengers and thirty minutes after boarding, the ferry blew her horn, ropes were slipped, and the engines pulled us gently away from shore. We navigated slowly down the Göta älv river. Along the shore were rows of freight yards and loading bays lined with large shipping containers and I smiled to myself thinking of the one I had shared with the Germans at Nordkapp only a few nights ago. As the estuary of the river widened, we passed under the elegant span of the

Älvsborgsbron road bridge and then the river widened dramatically and transitioned to open sea.

As we slipped into more open water, the wind increased from the west, but the air temperature remained pleasant. With the 17th century Nya Älvsborg Sea Fortress to port, a solitary bastion against a time when the Danes across the sea were far feistier and a whole lot less neighbourly, the note from the ferry's engines increased in pitch, and the bow was pushed through the low waves with increased gusto. Gothenburg slowly faded to a dark smudge behind us.

I was really enjoying relinquishing the navigating and responsibility of riding to the captain for a few hours. The boat rode the gentle swells with ease, and I was daydreaming of a cold pint in a warm hotel bar with my eyes half closed, sun on my pasty face, when a female voice roused me from my reverie.

"Do you please, to mind, if I buy you a coffee?"

The voice was soft and accented, Danish or Swedish, I couldn't tell which. I opened my eyes and looked at the woman. She was in her late twenties, doubly blessed with the genetics of her Scandinavian ancestors, she wore her blond hair short, in a pixie cut above soft blue eyes. She was smiling at me like we were old friends, or lovers even. In my initial confusion, I wasn't even sure it was me she was talking to so, like a fool, I looked quickly around to see who might be stood behind me.

There was nobody else remotely close by, so I pointed a finger at my chest and with a goofy expression asked, "who me?"

Her smile widened, showing perfect white teeth in a slight overbite, "yes. I would like for to buy a coffee to you, is it OK?"

I had no idea why she was talking to me. I was not generally the type of guy who beautiful female strangers approached. Not remotely. In fact, I was the one who occasionally approached a beautiful stranger only to be told, in a stern voice, to "fuck right off."

The sum of my life's experiences with the opposite sex had not exactly furnished my young self with a range of tools to effectively deal with this new curve ball. The situation was made much more puzzling to me as, when I took a moment to look at her properly, I found her to have a baby, nestled in the crook of one arm and feeding on an ample naked breast.

I was entirely nonplussed so just muttered in a voice pitched ridiculously high, "that would be nice, thank you."

She nodded, smiled again and quickly walked away towards the cafeteria inside the ship.

I was quite thrilled and as flattered as could be. While she was gone, I ran several utterly insane scenarios through my mind while she was absent. They were all terribly exciting and they all ended up with me moving to Denmark and living with this blonde supermodel. I just couldn't figure out how the baby factored into any of them.

She returned with two steaming Styrofoam cups in a cardboard carrier. I took one and she sat down, hips almost touching, next to me. I thought I might catch fire.

"My name, it is Clara by the ways." She put her coffee down and held out a small hand.

"Andy," I replied taking the proffered hand gently in mine. That first touch was electric, and I tingled all over. This was going so well, exactly how I had imagined.

In one of my insane daydreams, the next thing she would ask me was where I planned to stay in Denmark and would I like, instead, to go home with her, so I was more than a little bamboozled when she said.

"I am soon, in Frederickshavn, meeting to my husband, but I am studying of the English. Can we talk together for a while so I am learning better?"

It turned out my fortunes with the fairer sex had not in fact turned, and the baby was not going to be quite the problem I thought it might be. Clara was travelling to her home in Copenhagen and, as she had walked past me, she had seen the Union Jack sticker on the back of my helmet and decided to have a little language practice with the sad, prematurely balding, and tatty looking Englishman.

Still, we chatted for about an hour or so. About my trip and her gorgeous home by the sea in Copenhagen. But most of all Clara spoke about her tediously handsome and successful husband and her cute and babbling baby who, "already is almost being able to say mutter and farter like a two-year age persons."

By the time the ferry horn blew to announce our arrival in Frederikshavn I hated both the husband and the child with an intensity usually reserved for rapists and war criminals. I still reserved judgement on Clara, as deep down I thought I might still be in with a shot there.

DENMARK

It was late afternoon when I pulled into the large, paved but cracked car park of the Hotel Skæve Tårne on the very edge of Brande. The ride south through Denmark had been an uneventful and pleasant cruise through a mostly flat land of corn fields and rich pasture. Fat Friesian cows stood, marked like Rorschach tests, heads bowed to munch on the sweet grass. The weather had remained dry and warm, and I had made great speedy progress.

I had glimpsed the hotel from the dual carriageway through a gap in the trees. It fitted my requirements exactly. Slightly shabby exterior with a few broken windows and thistle filled flower beds. Its sorry condition was likely to match my equally threadbare budget.

I checked in and hauled my gear to a small room on the first floor. The room was as grubby, musty and dated as I had expected. It matched the exterior of the hotel and the price I had paid to a T. Its saving grace was that it did have its own tiny bathroom. The bathroom was the antithesis of a TARDIS, it being magically smaller on the inside than it appeared from the outside. But when I squeezed myself in and ran the shower, the water was hot, although the flow was as ferocious as a dripping tap. With some practice and a jiggle of the wobbly handle even the toilet eventually flushed.

As I began to lower my weight to the bed, the slats holding up the mattress creaked like a door in a haunted house and when I tested the comfort with the very slightest of bounces, the sharp crack of a support slat breaking made me jump. I got up to investigate and lifted the top blanket. Underneath the blanket, the duvet itself was thick and warm but around the top half that covered the torso were multiple holes and around each of the holes were dark stains. It looked all the world like the scene of a frenzied stabbing. When I lifted the duvet to check the mattress, I discovered how they had disposed of the bodies. All the little bedroom needed was some police tape and a coroner with a UV light.

I cared not a single jot. The room had a roof and a window, albeit too high to see out of, a semi-functional bed, an almost serviceable toilet, and a shower. Bloody luxury.

I was still having some stomach problems and had come to the slow realization that there might have been a loose connection between my lack of recent bowel movements and my intake of hard-boiled eggs. I was literally egg bound and didn't know what to do about it, other than to consume a steak dinner and wash it down with several Danish lagers to see if I could jiggle things loose again.

Down in the restaurant area I appeared to be the only guest, but the owner/manager was friendly and jovial and spoke excellent English. His name was Otto, and he was a dead ringer for Disney's idea of Geppetto, bushy white hair and moustache, a bulbous purple drinker's nose that held up circular wire rimmed spectacles with lenses so powerful his eyes blinked like huge China blue dinner plates behind them.

He seated me at a wobbly table, on a wobbly chair that felt like, if I moved in any way at all, like for example to cut up food, the joints might fail and deposit me on the floor.

I ordered the bøf og chips, medium rare, and a litre of Tuborg, the local lager. Geppetto must have carved the steak fresh from a piece of hardwood, as when it came it was as difficult to swallow as the whole story about Pinocchio being a real boy. Still, I was starving so I ate it all even though it made my teeth and jaws ache and washed it down with a beer so good I ordered another, and then another. With three litres of fizzy beer inside of me, I left the restaurant on wobbly legs. It took me a few goes to make the stairs and with a gurgling belly full of fries, lager, and overcooked beef I fell into a deep sleep on my murder bed.

In the morning, I boiled water in an electric kettle filled from a tap and made a coffee and drank it from an actual mug, sat on the end of a bed. It felt wonderful to have stowed the tent and my camping and cooking equipment. The coffee was even having an effect on my bowels, and I decided to test the capabilities, resilience and flushing capacity of the toilet.

Seldom has man, or woman, contended with such a fearsome and hefty foe. At first it seemed a battle un-winnable but with the first blockage cleared with pure brute force, the path was finally cleared and a smooth road laid. I had burst blood vessels in my eyes and threaded veins across my cheeks for a week or so, and I took care not to eat another egg for a month, but I felt immeasurably better and immediately hungry again.

Denmark was lovely in the summer. It was warm and the skies remained clear. I toured around the country for a bit of sightseeing, always ending up at my cheap hotel in the evening to eat a hearty, if charred and gristly piece of meat and then collapse, warm, happy, and fuzzy headed into my bed.

The day after my 'eggbound evacuation' I awoke with a veritable spring in my step. I woke early, cleaned the bike in the car park, with a sponge and a bucket filled with sudsy water borrowed from the hotel porter, and quickly set off to explore Copenhagen.

The bike rode like a dream with the tent and panniers all still stored in my hotel bedroom. I still had the tank bag in front of me so that I could read the Michelin map. I used the highways as Copenhagen was a three-hour ride in each direction. It was a long trip, but I didn't want to leave Denmark and not see at least something of the city.

I thought the countryside closely resembled northern France, but the air definitely had a Scandinavian tang of the sea to it. It was a beautiful country filled with small, neat towns and vast arable fields. I crossed the Vejle fjord on the long stretch of the Vejle Fjord Bridge. The fjord glittered icy blue and pretty in the sunshine. For a change I was bone dry and toasty warm and enjoying myself immensely.

I passed south of Odense and then at Nyborg I had to wait fifteen minutes for the large and very busy ferry to take me across the Samsø Bælt, or Great Belt which is the forty mile stretch of water that divides Denmark. There is a massive, modern bridge there now, but of course I chose to travel in a much slower but more romantic era. The ferry took me close to ninety minutes to cross the same distance that travellers can now complete in about ten.

Copenhagen sits to the very far east of the islands of Zealand and Amager but it wasn't long before I reached the outskirts of the city and instantly became hopelessly lost in its busy, ancient tangle of streets. My road map wasn't of a suitable scale for navigating a city, so I did what I always do when I am lost. I took four or five random turns and then finding a large diesel bus blocking my path, while it idled waiting for passengers to board, when it finally set off, I followed it.

The bus could have easily been on its way back to the depot in the suburbs as far as I was aware, but as chance would have it, its fourth stop was directly outside of the Tivoli gardens. I parked the bike next to several other smaller motorcycles on the pavement, and with helmet in hand I wandered aimlessly around wondering what I was looking at for a very happy hour.

I hadn't prepared myself for visiting Copenhagen in any way. I just liked the sound of the name of the place. No research, no library visit. No tour guides. I am certain I walked past the Opera House, the Frederiksberg Palace and Grundtvig's church, but if I did, I was blissfully unaware of it. The architecture was splendid though, and all of the people were pretty, young and smiling and it was a beautiful place to be for a little while.

I did stumble upon the statue of the Little Mermaid at the Langelinie Promenade. Even in my ignorant youth I had heard of that landmark. But it did seem to be very small indeed and it left me a little unimpressed. I don't seem to be the only visitor to feel that way, because the iconic statue has been beheaded several times.

With Copenhagen's rich culture and world-famous art mostly passing me by, I ate a Danish pastry and glugged a startlingly strong cup of coffee I bought from a street vendor for an alarming number of my dwindling coins. I had a very satisfying pee in the free public toilets of the Tivoli and jumped back on the bike. My stomach was grumbling for a piece of tough, sinewy, and overcooked steak, and I knew just where to get it.

The very next day I woke and decided to visit the most famous thing in Denmark. Not Danish pastries, salty liquorice or even Hans Christian Anderson. The most famous thing to visit in Denmark is Legoland. In 1989 when this tale took place, there was only one Legoland and you had to travel to Denmark, to the small of Billund, not very far from my hotel, to be precise, to visit it and to play with the Lego there. Today you are spoilt by choice. There are ten Legoland's, the original and I would argue, the best, is still located in Billund, but now there are others in California, Florida, New York, Malaysia, Dubai, Windsor, Japan, Korea and Germany.

I arrived early and parked the bike close to the entrance. The day was cool with a stiff breeze, but the sun still shone through the light smattering of thin clouds.

Legoland is what you would consider to be a proper theme park nowadays. One with log flumes and roller coasters. When I visited it was hardcore Lego. Just rows and rows of miniature Lego houses built around Lego harbours with Lego trains carrying Lego passengers to far away Lego locations. Well, you get the idea, there was a shit ton of Lego and not much else.

For most of the day I occupied myself just walking around marvelling at the little Lego lions and giraffes in Savannah land, Lego spaceships and UFOs in Space world, small Lego cowboys riding Lego horses and shooting at Lego Native Americans in Wild West world.

I have to say I had a lovely time, even though I did attract some unwanted attention from some of the parents, as I appeared to be the only male adult who was unaccompanied by children and dressed entirely in black leather. I must have looked for all the world like an escaped performer from a risqué Munich cabaret. All I needed were some chains and a little whip.

EINDHOVEN

I was only in Denmark for three days, but the respite from riding hundreds of miles every day through dreadful weather conditions and the restorative powers of a bed, albeit a decrepit and potentially stabby one, a simple roof over my head and steak dinners that refuelled my body and exercised my jaws had done wonders. I felt fitter and stronger and ready to carry on with the journey. I actually didn't have a choice anyway; I was due back at work in four days.

I packed my bike and set off on a beautiful midsummer morning. Geppetto and a couple of the kitchen porters came out to shake my hand and wave me a fond farewell. I had an easy ride through the low countries, south through Denmark to cross the northern coastal region of Germany and end the day at my good friend René's house in the town of Eindhoven in the Netherlands.

I rode close to the western coast as much as I could, through small medieval towns and villages, keeping away from the motorways and dual carriageways. The towns were pretty with half-timbered houses, affluent neighbourhoods and neat shops. The roads were smooth and well maintained, bicycle lanes running parallel to the road kept helmeted riders safe. Everything was neater than a pin, not a scrap of litter to be seen anywhere. It was very beautiful.

It was clear to me why the Danes generally come top, or very close to it, in rankings for the happiest country on the planet. They rank high for all the things that really matter in this tough life we lead, healthy life expectancy, GDP per capita, social support in times of trouble, low corruption, and high social trust. The opposite of 1980's Britain for sure, where the country of my birth had instead invested heavily in corruption in politics, sexual abuse in its churches, violence in the pubs, graffiti on the walls and as much free dog shit on your shoes as you could carry in the deep tread of a Doc Martin.

I stopped to show my passport to a German border guard and entered Germany around noon. The Germans might not be as deliriously happy as the Danes but by

God they are efficient. On the Autobahn I immediately saw a sign for a Rastplatz, a rest stop, and pulled over to refuel both myself and the bike. Finally, away from the Nordic countries I could afford things again. I popped inside the shopping centre and had a pee in a bathroom so large, sterile and decorated with glistening white tile and sparkling chromium I could have been in a vast operating theatre or mortuary.

The choice at the sandwich counter was restricted to various wursts, bratwurst, weisswurst, blutwurst, and leberwursts, all rolled onto split grainy buns and slathered with German mustard. I ordered a bratwurst and a coke and took it outside to sit in the sunshine by my bike.

It wasn't long before three German bikers pulled up to park alongside me. Unlike the feral crew from Nordkapp these were of the more typical European variety. Tall and well-groomed with top of the range BMW motorcycles, brand new gear and matching leathers that had never been used in anger. I looked down at the torn patch of leather on my right shoulder, the mud so deeply ingrained on my leather trousers and boots it had become a perma-nent fixture, the scratched visor and helmet still sporting the blood streaks from the killer mosquitos Georgie and Ella and I had had to endure near Kautokeino. My bike's fairing was scratched and cracked and covered with the detritus of too many days on the road and the bodies of one-hundred-thousand insects. We looked each other up and down for a second.

"Where is it you are coming from," one of the Germans finally asked.

I took a deep breath, it felt like talking about something sacred, a life experience I was suddenly reluctant to share with these fair-weather boys and their fancy expensive toys.

"Nordkapp."

The group nodded with understanding now in their eyes.

"Nordkapp, wow. It is very far."

One of the other said something about the 'Polarkreises' which I assume meant the arctic circle and I nodded sagely, the very epitome of the experienced but world-weary traveller to distant lands. They all looked suitably impressed and took a respectful step back to provide me with the appropriate amount of respect due.

"Well, I gotta be going guys."

They watched me pull on and buckle my helmet and zip up my tatty leather jacket. I swung a leg over the bike and pulled in the clutch to hit the starter button. The bike started with its familiar deep burble and as I nodded farewell, they all raised a hand in salute, arms a little too extended for my complete comfort. I felt like Roald

Amundsen returning amid Norwegian celebrations from his Arctic expeditions.

That was until, in my effort to live up to the hype of my toughness and expertise gleaned through hard won adventure, I gunned the throttle hard and leant the bike over to the left in what I had planned to be a loud and impressive sweep out of the car park. Unfortunately, in my haste I had left the kickstand down and it now dug into the tarmac and sent me wobbling, accompanied by a loud shriek, back over to my right. I now made a series of increasingly desperate corrections, weaving madly down the road, handlebars slapping uncontrollably from right to left and left to right like some giant comical metronome, until I managed to finally get the bike stopped. Breathing hard and blushing furiously I quickly swept the kickstand up and out of the way, and without a backward glance I accelerated the bike and re-joined the Autobahn.

I rode hard and fast for the rest of the day, taking advantage of the sections of Autobahn, always outside any city limits, that have no speed restrictions. The Kawasaki was a joy, responsive and nimble and I touched speeds of up to 140 mph without having to be concerned about the police. It's surprising how far down the road your eyes and attention need to be focused at those speeds.

It wasn't long before I had to slow to join the westbound Autobahn close to Hamburg. The ride west was dull and repetitive, the country low and fertile but busy and congested with commuter traffic. I passed Bremen and dealt with the Dutch border procedures near to the town of Zwartemeer. Past the towns of Arnhem and Nijmegen I rode now mostly south, tired, and weary and finally, with the sun beginning to set, a lipstick smear of crimson clouds across the neat, tiled roofs of the town, I pulled up with relief to park the bike, popping and ticking, onto the smart and tidy concrete drive of Rene's home in the suburbs of Eindhoven.

STRATUMSEIND

I had met Rene when he was on a kind of work experience in the UK. He was a young and recently graduated industrial chemist. He worked at Philips, the gargantuan consumer electrical and lighting conglomerate based in Eindhoven. Philips had given him the opportunity to work at the Philips factory located in Southport where I lived. My brother worked there at the time, and he befriended him and brought him to our weekly pub sessions. Rene was good looking, tall and athletic and spoke with a fanny fluttering Dutch accent that the girls in the nightclubs we frequented just couldn't resist.

In the evenings we would go to the YMCA first and do circuit training and lift weights and then go to the nightclub. Rene would immediately be surrounded by beautiful girls. I hung about like an ugly sister hoping to catch one of the girls who didn't quite make the grade and, who I hoped, was on the sweeter side of desperate. I would like to say he was an asshole, which many good-looking guys can be, but he was sweet and smart and funny and everybody, men, and women together, all loved him.

I was only going to be in Eindhoven for a few nights so in the morning as we ate a breakfast of scrambled eggs and some sort of toast that had the consistency of cardboard, I asked him what we should do for the day. It turned out I was in luck. The summer fair was in town. But first we needed transport.

There is no single reason why the Dutch embraced the bicycle more than almost any other nation. An amazing thirty-six percent of Dutch people list the bicycle as their primary mode of transport. The country is flat and cool of course which helps, but perhaps the biggest driver is the investment by the government in dedicated bicycle lanes and training.

There was a move away from cycles and an increase of car usage in the 1970's but the Dutch population, led by a lady called Maartje van Putten, brought the people together when child deaths on the roads began to rise. Called the Stop de Kindermoord ('*Stop the Child Mur-*

der'), it turned government policy around. I think we all need more Maartje's in our lives.

Rene of course already had a bicycle, but we needed to walk a few blocks to his friend's house to borrow a bicycle for me. We arrived around noon and walked up the stairs to the apartment. Inside I was introduced to some of Rene's friends, who we would meet up with later. I was a tad concerned, as all of Rene's friends were all around six foot five inches tall and I top out at an unimpressive five foot nine. In motorcycle boots. On tippy toes.

Sure enough when we got the bike, a black framed and heavy utilitarian bicycle that might have been owned by a postman during the second world war, onto the pavement, I found that I could ride it, but only with quite a degree of difficulty. By lowering the handlebars and saddle as far as they would physically go, I found that I could just push the pedals with the very tips of my big toes, but had to lean the bike far over to one side when I stopped pedalling so that I could keep one foot on a pedal and reach with a twitching foot to dab the ground with the other.

We cycled into the town centre and left the bikes unlocked close to the Karaokebar Ameezing next to the Dommel Canal.

"Wont our bicycles be stolen." I asked.

"Have you seen the bicycles we all ride?" Rene answered.

I looked around at the racks upon racks of bicycles. They were all the same as mine, black with thick, heavy frames, the sort used by a 1930's delivery boy in a Hovis advert. Not a single shiny racing bike or mountain bike anywhere.

"But still…" Petty crime was rife in the UK. It didn't require somebody to steal your bicycle because they wanted it, they just didn't want you to have it.

"If they steal our bikes, we just take another one. They are all the same. And every year the city dredges the canal and like a thousand bicycles are pulled out of the canal. Then you can come and choose a new one," he laughed.

Rene ordered a couple of beers from a street bar, "twee Trappist alstublieft."

"Trappist?" I asked.

"It is a beer brewed only by the Trappist monks who live at the Brouwerij de Koningshoeven abbey in Holland. It is strong. You will like it."

The beer was served in a glass shaped like a shallow bowl. The beer was the colour of copper and the frothy head was thick and creamy. The taste was tangy and filled with the flavours of hops and caramel. I could feel the effects of the beer even as I drank it. I picked up the bottle the barman had placed on the counter.

"Nine percent! Shit, I'm pissed already."

Rene just laughed, "not yet, but you will be."

In the square by the neo-gothic church of Sint Cathari-nakerk a fun fair had been set up with carousels and street entertainers. Music blared, the Eurovision type, all twangy, happy guitars and foreign lyrics barely squeezed in to match the tune. Jugglers juggled and clowns scared. We bought another beer and turned the corner into the Stratumseind.

The Stratumseind is the longest pub street in the Netherlands. A quarter of a kilometre long, quite narrow in places and filled with bars, cafés, and eateries, mostly shawarma outlets. I had been here before although my memories were a little alcohol hazed and fractured. But today was different, for some strange reason the street was thickly covered in straw.

"What is going on?" I asked.

"Come, lets walk to the end of the street and I will show you."

We walked slowly down the street enjoying the smell of the food, the beer and the cannabis that was being bought from the cafes and smoked freely and without care. It was mid-afternoon and the place was already buzzing, and so was I.

By the time night fell I knew this place would be crazy, packed, and loud with voices, lights and music. When we got to the end of the street the reason for the straw was revealed, first by smell and then by sight. Stood, penned between tall bales of hay facing back down the street were two full size male camels. On the backs of the camels, between humps, were small and uncomfortable saddles. A sign next to the bales advertised "Kameel Racen." A long line of willing, but clearly inebriated and amateur Camel jockeys was lined up waiting to race each other.

A horn blew, two drunken Dutchmen were hoisted onto the backs of the truly enormous camels, the crowd along the street parted and the camels were let go. They shot out of their pens, eight camel toes splayed onto the cobbled street, all cheered on by the crowd. The Dutch boys were flung wildly backwards and forwards, heads snapping from spine to chest, eyes wide and knuckles white, as the camels galloped crazily down the Stratum-seind, cloven hooves flying in every direction. The crowds along the street whooped and hollered and the Camels ran faster, threatening to dislodge their jockeys with their loping, awkward gait until they disappeared out of sight.

It was such a typically, strangely Dutch thing to see. Such an enigma the Dutch. So much like the Germans in many ways (although, for good reasons I wouldn't be thanked for saying so), orderly, organized and regimented in so many facets of their lives and the manner in which they build and manage cities, adhere to rules and regulations, they are all seemingly professional and well educated. But also, so left of centre, quirky and unpredictable. The Dutch have embraced the legalization of drugs, prostitution, and euthanasia. Instead of banning these things and forcing them underground where they become sordid, dirty, expensive and dangerous, they have regulated them, made them (for the most part) a normal part of life and built a better society with the tax money derived from them.

And then, of course, there is letting drunks race camels down a busy pedestrian street during the middle of the day.

Later on, as night fell and the sun was replaced by the sodium streetlights and the neon from the bars, Rene's lofty friends joined us to make me feel like a rickets crippled hobbit.

I don't remember much of that drunken, beer and cannabis fuelled night. There were a myriad of bars, kebabs and hilarity. Shouting, singing, smoking and then more drinking. In and out of endless bars, we made our slow and increasingly wobbly way from one end of the Stratumseind to the other. We ended the night in a swirl of dizzying smoky lights and blaring sounds that swooped and rose and dove around us, and then we staggered out of the last bar and into the cold of the pre-dawn of the next day.

I do remember climbing back onto my much too tall bicycle and pedalling home along streets long deserted, and I do remember not realizing how high I was, both in terms of distance from pavement and detachment of brain, when we had to stop at a red light. I kept my left foot on one peddle and lowered my right, but the curb I thought to be there was, in fact, not. My foot twitched for a second in empty air and then in the slowest of motions, me and the bicycle tilted over. The top of my head described a perfect 90 degrees arc, and I crashed to the ground in a messy tangle of limbs handlebars and spokes. Rene dismounted his bicycle, doubled up with tears of hysterical laughter, and helped me back up. We pushed our bicycles the last half mile home.

ANTWERP

I woke with a scratch, a groan and a fart so robust that it immediately silenced the pigeons cooing outside my window. I took a moment to do a quick system check. Headache, not too crippling. All fingers and toes present and wiggling, all limbs moving, both eyes functional. I felt surprisingly good all things considered. I had a large, fresh bruise the colour of an eggplant on the inside of my thigh from where I had landed on the frame of the bicycle, and my mouth was as dry as an Arab's sandal, but I had slept until almost noon. I was in good shape.

Ah, to be twenty-four again, blessed with the almost miraculous powers of recuperation I once possessed. Nowadays, if I had drunk half of what I had drunk that night, all those years ago down the Stratumseind, you would have had to roll me into A&E in a wheelbarrow and let me sleep for a week.

Anyway, the day was wasting, and we had a trip planned. Over our ninth or tenth Trappist beer, in the dark corner of some bar or another, Rene had convinced me that we should ride to Antwerp and spend the night camping there, close to the city, and enjoy a quiet and refined glass or two of some refreshing beverages, while we toured that fair city.

An hour later, after some fresh orange juice and a greasy breakfast of fried eggs and some sliced rookwurst, a delicious smoked pork sausage, Rene finally found a dusty motorcycle helmet in the storage under the stairs. He had borrowed it from a friend and had forgotten to return it. It was a touch on the small side and puffed his cheeks out like a hamster and gave him a headache, but we only had an hour to ride. We saddled up and set off.

We stuck to the main roads but avoided the Autobahns. The day was fine and warm, and the traffic was light. The countryside entirely flat but very pretty, low woods on the horizon and vast dazzlingly yellow fields of rape on either side. We passed through small sleepy towns that reminded me of Denmark, trim houses on neat birch lined streets. Entire families of cyclists out enjoying the weather, heading to play in parks and learn in schools.

We crossed into Belgium without issue and were soon on the outskirts of Antwerp itself. Rene knew of a campsite that was within walking distance of the town centre, so we parked up the bike, put up the tent and, given it was now early afternoon and we hadn't had a drink in nearly eight hours, we decided to walk in to town to get a beer.

We took seats at a small cast iron table outside a bar in the Grote Markt, the large central square located in the heart of the old city quarter. Now, I take my beer drinking pretty seriously but the Belgium's arc on another planet. The waiter, an old bent over guy with a bristling black moustache came over and presented us each with a leatherbound tome, each over an inch and a half-thick, handed over with the same reverence you might associate with an original copy of the bible.

Inside were descriptions and pictures of the hundred or so beers on sale. We began our little soiree with a Kriek beer. The description read like one of those snobby wine merchant magazines—*an easy drinking and intense, tart, cherry-sweet lambic fruit beer. Good with venison and meat balls. ABV 3.7%.* The waiter brought out the Kriek branded beer mats and placed the Kriek branded glasses containing our pink beverages on the table. We had taken the menu's advice and also ordered some meatballs, and they arrived just as we took our first sips. It was a good thing we had the salty meatballs to take away the taste of the cherry flavoured beer, I found it to be spine shudderingly awful.

We decided to mix it up by ordering a round of Kwak beers—*A strong amber ale served in a miniature yard-of-ale glass supported by a wooden stand. ABV 8.4%.*

The waiter came and removed our Kriek branded beer mats and replaced them with beer mats proudly displaying the Kwak brand, and then a minute or so later, brought out our little wooden stands that supported the narrow neck, and held upright, the round bottomed glasses containing our dark amber beverages. I took a deep draught and almost immediately regretted it; this was seriously strong stuff. I had to pat the table with my palm and blink three times to restore my sight.

Our next choice was a Rochefort 10—*of the Trappist family, a rich, fruity, dark caramelly nutty beer, great with dark fruit cake or chocolate. ABV 11.3%.*

We didn't have any fruit cake or chocolate, but the waiter served the beer with the same deference and respect as all of the other beers. The light was beginning to seep from the sky when we moved bars. We didn't have to go far, there were tens of them, all clustered around the imposing visage of the neo-gothic Provincial Court building.

We drank a Westmalle, a Westmalle Dubbel and a Westmalle Tripel, the very trifecta of Westmalle's, and then moved on again, a little less steady now, to drink an Orval, a Leffe and a Hoegaarden. We paused at around ten o'clock for hamburgers, served bloody as they should be in Europe, stopped at a bureau de change to replenish our dwindling supplies of beer tokens and then found an inside bar to settle in for the night, as the air was becoming cold and crisp.

We ordered more beers, I had long since stopped taking note of what they were at that late stage, the waiter brought us a dinner menu and we ordered more meatballs. The bar became crowded, and we became lost in our little world as the conversation went on around us. The conversations were mostly in Flemish, a form of Dutch, some French and occasionally a smattering of German. They are all spoken in Belgium to some degree, and of course, many people are multi-lingual as are many others in the areas known as the low country. I of course, being English, spoke none.

The beers kept coming and we kept drinking them. The crowd faltered and then dispersed, and we suddenly found ourselves drinking alone. The bar keeper was sweeping the floor and stacking chairs on top of tables. I glanced out of the window and was startled to see the smudge of light breaking over the ancient, tiled roofs of the gothic architecture. Time to go.

We walked back through a city just beginning to wake. We passed a street cleaner, whistling his way down the cobbled streets, broom in hand, leaving a smoky trail from the cigarette that dangled from his lips. We could hear the call of the gulls as they followed the returning fishing smacks only a few miles to our north.

We stumbled, thankfully into the campsite, found our tent and like sleepwalking zombies we climbed into sleeping bags and fell into a deeply drunken sleep.

Home Again, Home Again

I t was very late in the morning by the time we began to come alive and return from the state our refined "glass or two" had rendered us into. The temperature in the tent was stifling and so was the odour of our two bodies as we shed sweat and alcohol fumes in equal measure. It was time to leave before we incurred another night's charge for camping.

We had seen almost nothing of the ancient city of Antwerp, with the exception of the outside of fifteen bars and a handful of the inside of others. But I was content. It had been fun. But now it was time to ride carefully back to Eindhoven. I only had one more night to spend there. Work urgently called to me from across the channel.

I needed to catch the ferry the next day and get back to the UK in time for work on Monday morning.

With pounding heads, we found the campsite shop and bought some Lucozade. It was the morning pick me up of its day for the borderline alcoholic, sweet with glucose and full of electrolytes, it was even issued by the NHS to patients in hospitals in the 1970's as a restorative for the sick. We took a quick shower and feeling almost human again we packed up the tent and loaded up the bike. Rene squeezed his sore head into the too tight helmet, and we were off.

The ride back to Rene's house was uneventful although I felt queasy all the way and was terrified that I might throw up into my full-face helmet and drown like a rat, fallen headfirst into a fishbowl full of diced carrots. But the day was warm and pretty and weekend traffic was light. We arrived back around dinner time and, exhausted, we both crashed in our rooms for an hour or so. Around eight in the evening, with the sun just starting to lose its warmth we bicycled back into town and found a quiet bar to enjoy the last night together.

We enjoyed a quiet and fairly civilized evening, tucked away in some corner of a darkened bar talking about all of the good times we had shared in the UK. We managed to reign in our baser impulses and returned to the house at a respectable midnight, to fry up some eggs and then roll into our respective beds.

In the morning, I did some basic checks and maintenance on the bike, checked the oil, tire pressures, and tightened and lubricated the chain. All was good. I packed my things back onto the bike and said my farewells to Rene. We didn't get to see each other much anymore. A day or two every other year or so at most. That's life, I guess. Time moves relentlessly forwards and leaves the travellers on its fast-flowing stream behind, stranded on one side of the bank or the other. Ties and bonds become stretched to breaking. I didn't know it then, but the next time I would see Rene would be at his wedding, and the time after that, he at mine.

But that time was still a little further down the stream. We waved our goodbyes as I pulled the bike out of his drive and set off towards the port of Calais.

It was a tedious three-hour ride through the worst of northern Holland, Belgium and France. The roads there were always crammed with haulage traffic, large trucks and articulated lorries and the skyline is seldom free of the dark towers and angled cranes of industrialization and urbanization. Back around Antwerp, onwards to Ghent, crossing into France near Dunkirk and then along the crowded and industrial coast road to the port itself. There was no tunnel between England and France in those days, but the ferries were cheap at the time and ran on a regular basis.

I always enjoyed the ferry. It took a perfectly suitable amount of time in my opinion to get from France to England. The channel tunnel is too fast and sterile. Inside the Chunnel you are deprived a view, and you simply don't have time to consider or mentally adjust to the fact that you will soon be in a different country and driving on the other side of the road and failing to speak a foreign language, especially true if you land in Newcastle.

The ferry takes roughly a leisurely hour and a half to get back across the Channel to Dover and good old blighty. You have time to secure the bike and pop upstairs to get a pint or a sandwich, or both. You can stand on the deck with the wind whipping the last of your hair away in the stiff breeze and try to avoid having seagulls steal your cheese and onion crisps.

I made it to Calais around noon and soon found a ferry scheduled to leave within the hour. It was preparing to board, and I already had a reservation, so I rode to the front of the line of queuing cars. The boarding doors were already open, displaying the cavernous steel interior of the roll on/roll off ship. I wrote about the Herald of Free Enterprise ferry disaster in '*A Fast Bike to Byzantium*,' so wont recount the tale of the disaster here but waiting to board definitely made the nerves tingle and my mouth run dry with trepidation.

A horn blared and one of the boarding agents waved me forward. Up the iron ramp and into the bowels of the ship I went. I secured the bike and climbed the steel stairs to find the cafeteria and some lunch. Certain that there was still a substantial amount of Dutch beer swilling and circulating through my veins I opted for the bacon sandwich and a piping, steaming hot coffee. I stood on the deck of the ship and, as the ships klaxon sounded, I watched the lines slip and the water at her stern churn and froth under the power of the huge diesel engines.

There is something magical about seeing the white cliffs of dover hove into view. A long white signal flare strung out below a roof of verdant meadow. It sang a sweet song of home and all that that truly means. A return to safety and security, the familiar and the comfortable.

But also, a deep sadness. A journey ended. An adventure curtailed. The somewhat unwelcome conclusion of weeks of just winging it, of following a random red line on a Michelin map to somewhere unknown based on the whisper of a stranger. Sleeping on the damp bracken bed of an empty campsite. A random laugh shared with a fellow biker met in the middle of absolutely fucking nowhere. The fear, the thrill, the gut-wrenching loneliness, and the pure exhilaration of the open road. A final destination known, but a path invented and re-invented ten times a day.

The ferry slowly docked and as I felt it bump up against the buffers of the dock. I considered my adventure over. I still had a five-hour ride to get back to my hometown, but it already felt like I was done with the hard work, the long journey behind me.

I left the M58 near Wigan close to seven in the evening. The sun was getting low in the candy floss coloured sky, setting flame to the clouds, reds and purples streaked across the horizon to the west. Red sky in the morning, sailors warning, red sky at night, Birkenhead is on fire, as the local saying went.

I rode through the busy market town of Ormskirk, concentrating hard.

I had read, in a motorcycle magazine, that on a long-distance journey, the last ten miles for a motorcyclist are by the far most dangerous. It's when you let your guard down. Riding familiar roads, roads you have ridden all of your life, you know all of the junctions, all of the potholes, all of the raised and slippery manhole covers. Nearly home, you relax, you stop all of the non-stop scanning for all of the usual hazards that can end the journey and sometimes life of a two-wheeled journeyman. Cars about to pull out of junctions, slippery white lines, pedestrians blindly blundering into streets, cats, dogs, more cars pulling out of junctions. It is amazing how heightened your senses become when riding a motorcycle and it can quickly become exhausting.

I saw the familiar outline of the Gas storage tower, the Gasometer as we called it, a tall blue thumb towering above the skyline of my hometown of Southport. Mum was waiting for me anxiously and when she heard the bike pull onto her drive, she ran out. After a hard hug she immediately went into the kitchen to make me some tea.

I carefully parked the Kawasaki. It had been quite the ride, eight different countries, close to five-thousand miles, the very worst of summer weather the Arctic Circle had to offer and far too much beer with Rene. In hindsight after all of the challenging miles, drenching rains and the crash with Georgie, it might have been the Belgian beer that nearly killed me. The bike riding was fine, but that Kriek beer. Hurp.

I gave the seat of the Kawasaki a friendly pat. We had been there for each other. Two silent companions who had dared to venture and finally win through. This ride had been one of my hardest. I had lost weight on the road. I had already been thin, but now I looked like a prisoner liberated from Belsen.

I kept in touch with Georgie for a few years. Initially by snail mail and then, when it was invented and made available to the general public, by email. We promised to meet up again sometime soon, maybe next year or the year after that. Perhaps go on a bike trip together to the South of France or Spain, somewhere warm, not anywhere near the bloody Arctic Circle. Of course, over time, we stopped emailing. When I decided to write this book, I searched every folder and old email accounts for his contact details, hoping to chat with him about our adventure, but I couldn't find anything that would help me locate him.

He and Ella have become living ghosts on the pages of the book that you hold in your hands. I hope they are well and still together, married now perhaps with lots of little square headed Georgie's and ebony-haired Ella's running around and worrying their parents by buying motorcycles and setting off to crazy, far-flung destinations. But to me they have become fond, but slowly fading memories of a journey I am extremely glad I completed, but also very content to have in my past.

Thank you so much for the read—it is genuinely appreciated. If you enjoyed the tale, it would be very kind of you to leave a review on your favorite bookstore.

Read my other travel motorcycle adventures by following the links below to your local Amazon store.

A FAST BIKE TO BYZANTIUM

https://geni.us/BM_Byzantium

A FAST BIKE TO EVERYWHERE ELSE

https://geni.us/BM_FastBiketoEvery

A FAST BIKE THROUGH THE BADLANDS

https://geni.us/FastBikeBadlands

Please take a moment to visit my website to see more books and get great discounts and offers.

You can find me at www.andycwareing.com

ANDY C WAREING

ANDY C WAREING

Andy is a multi-genre Indie author, originally from the United Kingdom. He has lived with his wife Paula and their two dogs Archie and Pi in Atlanta GA for the last fifteen years (with the exception of a year in Spain/UK during the pandemic). At heart always British, he loved living in the U.S.A. but will never vocalize the American pronunciations of basil, banana, or tomato. He currently lives in leafy Somerset, a land of apples, cider, and weather so perpetually wet, 'wellies' are considered formal wear.

Please take a moment to visit my website to see more books and get great discounts and offers.

You can find me at www.andycwareing.com

ANDY C WAREING

Be a stalker and follow me on Facebook, Goodreads, or my author page on Amazon for updates on new projects:

facebook.com/andycwareing

amazon.com/author/andycwareing

g

goodreads.com/author/show/21017809.Andy_C_Warei ng

Printed in Great Britain
by Amazon

53702697R00116